BOBBY'S OPEN

BOBBY'S OPEN

Mr Jones and the Golf Shot that Defined a Legend

STEVEN REID

CORINTHIAN BOOKS

FH

Published in the UK and USA in 2012 by
Corinthian Books, an imprint of
Icon Books Ltd, Omnibus Business Centre,
39–41 North Road, London N7 9DP
email: info@iconbooks.co.uk
www.iconbooks.co.uk

Sold in the UK, Europe, South Africa and Asia
by Faber & Faber Ltd, Bloomsbury House,
74–77 Great Russell Street, London WC1B 3DA or their agents

Distributed in the UK, Europe, South Africa and Asia
by TBS Ltd, TBS Distribution Centre, Colchester Road
Frating Green, Colchester CO7 7DW

Published in Australia in 2012
by Allen & Unwin Pty Ltd,
PO Box 8500, 83 Alexander Street,
Crows Nest, NSW 2065

Distributed in Canada
by Penguin Books Canada,
90 Eglinton Avenue East, Suite 700,
Toronto, Ontario M4P 2Y3

Distributed to the trade in the USA
by Consortium Book Sales and Distribution,
The Keg House, 34 Thirteenth Avenue NE, Suite 101,
Minneapolis, MN 55413-1007

ISBN: 978-190685-028-9

Typeset in New Baskerville by Scribe Design

Printed and bound in the UK by
Clays Ltd, St Ives plc

Dedicated to my parents:
to my father Donald for the infinite patience and
tolerance he showed whilst introducing me to golf and
to my mother Joan for her endless giving.

Contents

List of figures and plates

Images in the text

Plate section

Foreword

by Jack Nicklaus

In *Bobby's Open* there are two chief characters: one a golf course; the other one of history's most outstanding golfers. As I have had the privilege of knowing both of them, I was delighted to be invited to contribute a foreword.

The golf course is the links layout of the Royal Lytham and St Anne's Golf Club. In 1963, and at the age of 23, I was on the brink of winning my first British Open when my youthful inexperience, combined with the fiendishly difficult last four holes at Royal Lytham denied me that chance. A week later, I won my first PGA Championship but the lessons learned at Royal Lytham dwelled with me for years to come. During that week and subsequent visits for Opens and the Ryder Cup, I came to greatly admire and respect the way the course tests a player's complete game. Although I never won an Open there, I came to recognise the thorough examination it presents to a player aspiring to win there.

The golfer is the unique and iconic Bob Jones.

I grew up idolising Mr Jones, first learning of his name and achievements from my father and other members at Scioto Country Club, the club in Columbus, Ohio, where I not only learned to play the game of golf as a boy but where Mr Jones won the 1926 US Open. While my awareness of him was keen due to the stories that had endured more than a quarter-century since that victory, my first meeting with Bob Jones came when I was fifteen years old and playing in the US Amateur in 1955. I remember that as I was walking off the eighteenth green of my final practice round on the James River Course at the Country Club of Virginia, someone called me over and said, 'Mr Jones would like to meet you.' I walked over, and he said, 'Young man, I've been sitting behind this green here for the last couple of hours, and there have been only a few people reach this green in two, and you were one of them. I wanted to congratulate you.' That evening, Bob Jones was the speaker at the banquet and at one point he said to me that he was going to come out and watch my first match. The nerves that accompany a fifteen-year-old playing in his first national amateur were already a bit exposed, especially when facing the formidable Bob Gardner, who went on to play in the Walker Cup, World Cup, and many other international amateur events. I actually had Bob down one hole after ten holes, despite anxiously awaiting the arrival of Mr Jones. All of sudden, coming down the tenth fairway, was Bob Jones. All I could think was, 'Oh my goodness.' He followed me for three holes, during which I went bogey-bogey-double bogey and went from one up in my match to two down. Sensing that his presence was affecting my game, he showed great consideration and thoughtfulness by turning to my father and said, 'I don't believe I'm doing young Jack much good. I think I'd better get out of here.' Although I lost on the last green, I took away a great impression of his sensitivity and concern.

I had the pleasure of seeing Bob Jones on many occasions after that. The most memorable, of course, was each time I went to Augusta National – a place that has always been very special to me, a mystique only enhanced by the history and the aura of Bob Jones, and what he meant to Augusta National and The Masters Tournament. I never actually saw Bob Jones play golf, which is a source of personal regret. Yet from film footage and the mental images I have created from so many conversations with people who knew him well, it is clear he had a swing that could be described as a work of art. Just as important as his technique was his ability to compete and win under the immense pressure he imposed on himself.

So much has been said, written and celebrated about Bob Jones, but in these pages there is a new overview on how he overcame self-admitted problems to achieve such greatness and become a standard by which many other champions, including my own career, were measured. The entire 1926 Championship is brought back to life in these pages. The book allows readers to travel with Bob Jones as he struggled with his game before finally hitting that justly celebrated shot at the 71st hole. It was a shot that summed up Jones as a man as well as a golfer.

During my early years playing in the Masters in the 1960s, my father and I used to treasure the time we spent talking with him in the Jones Cabin. He thought and cared deeply about the game, and with the publication in this book of the previously unknown letters from Jones to Royal Lytham, written in 1958, there is a glimpse into the keen enquiring mind that stayed with him despite his illness and an awareness of his enduring humanity.

Bob Jones was in so many ways a remarkable golfer and man. This book rightly presents him as such to the reader of today.

Preface

This is not just another book about Bobby Jones. Let's be honest, there is no need for 'just another book' about Bobby Jones. Instead it fits into a new genre of 'Openography', telling the story of how one Open Championship unfolded and evolved. In the case of the 1926 British Open played at Royal Lytham & St Anne's Golf Club, this account is also inevitably about one golfer, Robert Tyre Jones Jnr.

In examining how he came to win at St Anne's, it is revealing to review Jones's first transatlantic crossing and to trace in detail how he solved his earlier problems with temperament. From 1926 onwards he was to become the perfect winning machine and established a record that will never be equalled.

In the qualifying round for the British Open, Jones played at Sunningdale what is judged by many to have been the most nearly perfect round ever completed. Contemporary accounts give a flavour of the impact on those fortunate enough to have witnessed it.

The newspaper accounts of the time give a full account of the happenings during a memorable championship at St Anne's, encapsulated by the famous shot from sand at the 71st hole that gave Jones his victory.

The discovery of previously unknown correspondence between the club and Jones in 1958 reveals the extent of his inquiring mind that stayed alert despite his crippling illness.

As it is hoped that the book will be of interest on both sides of the Atlantic, the Open (as it is known to British readers) is described throughout as the British Open, notwithstanding the dismay this will generate in traditionalists on one side of the Atlantic! For similar reasons the Amateur will be described as the British Amateur. Bernard Darwin will be spinning in his grave.

In adult life, Jones disliked being called Bobby, being known as Robert by his mother, Rob by his father, Bob by his friends, Bub by his grandchildren and occasionally Rubber Tyre by a playful O.B. Keeler. It is because he was universally known by the golfing public as 'Bobby' that he will be referred to as such in this work.

The place Jones came to occupy in the world of golf is delightfully revealed in the account given by Sidney L. Matthew in *The Life and Times of Bobby Jones*. He describes the experience of Jones's long-standing friend, Robert W. Woodruff, when playing the Old Course at St Andrews. He was rather pleased when at the fifth hole he reached the front of the par-five fifth green in three shots. Turning to his rather 'crusty old caddie' he was foolish enough to say, 'That was three pretty good shots, don't you think?' The caddie responded, 'When I caddied for Bobby Jones, he was here in two.' Inadvisedly the golfer mischievously retorted, 'Who's Bobby Jones?' Woodruff recounted how 'The caddy could only stare at me, back off a step, then another, taking the golf bag off his shoulder and laying it on the ground as he continued to pace still further backwards incredulously. The caddy then turned towards the clubhouse and he never looked back.' Woodruff recalled, 'And he didn't come back.'

Ecce homo – behold the man.

Steven Reid, St Anne's 2012

CHAPTER ONE

'My, but you're a wonder, sir!'

It is not often that anything good comes out of the mouth of a caddie, but from time to time an utterance captures an occasion perfectly.

By 1936, it was getting on for six years since Bobby Jones had retired from competitive golf. He had reached the summit of the game by winning all four major championships – the British Open, British Amateur, US Open, US Amateur – in 1930, thereby triumphing in the events that made up what had been first described as the Impregnable Quadrilateral and subsequently, in more familiar terms, as the Grand Slam.

He had crossed the Atlantic once more with his wife Mary to attend the 1936 Olympics, held in Berlin as clouds gathered over Europe. His fellow travellers were the writer Grantland Rice and Robert Woodruff, along with their wives. After the sailing across the Atlantic, they broke their journey to Germany by spending a few days in Britain. Although Jones's game was indifferent, he had brought his clubs with him and accepted Woodruff's invitation to spend some time in Gleneagles, Scotland. To his delight his golf improved and after shooting two rounds of 71 his spirits lifted.

At dinner that evening, Jones's mind wandered and he felt the call of the 'Old Lady' of St Andrews. Surely he could not drive past the Old Course and not return to pay his respects? Accordingly a chauffeur was dispatched to enter his name and that of Woodruff for an afternoon round. The next day, Jones and Woodruff enjoyed a lunch with Norman Boase, then captain of the Royal and Ancient Golf Club (known to golfers everywhere simply as the R&A). Ten years earlier Boase had been chairman of the R&A's Championship Committee that had organised the holding of the Open Championship at Royal Lytham & St Anne's and by happy coincidence had led the young Jones out to the presentation ceremony after his win there.

At St Andrews, Boase had arranged for Willie Auchterlonie, winner of the Open in 1893, and Gordon Lockhart, professional at Gleneagles, to play with Jones and Woodruff. When Jones came down from lunch, he was concerned to see a large crowd of some 2,000 was around the first tee. Perhaps he had inadvertently chosen a day when some large tournament was being played? It was worse than that – he realised that the crowd was there to watch him!

Someone had noticed the name R.T. Jones Jnr on the drawsheet. The word had spread like wildfire through the auld grey town. Thousands abandoned their tasks and wandered down to the course. Shopkeepers heard the news and many closed up for the day. One left a note on his shop door explaining why his shop was mysteriously closed. The note simply said, 'Bobby's back.'

As the match got underway and the golfers headed away from the clubhouse, the crowd continued to grow and Rice estimated that it reached 6,000. Without any marshalling, an element of chaos was inevitable as the match struggled to make its way out down the course. Thankfully the crowd lifted Jones's game and after birdies at the second, the fifth and the sixth, he came to the eighth tee where he hit a soft four-iron shot that rolled back the years. Hit with a delicate fade, the ball cut around the mound that protected the pin and came to rest just eight feet from the flag. What happened next had remained a personal internal memory with Jones, until he revealed it in his book *Golf is My Game* published in 1961. Perhaps sensing the escalating problems with his health and aware that this book was likely to be 'my last utterance on the subject of golf', he overcame his innate modesty to share that experience with others: as he put the club back into the bag, the caddie, a young man in his early twenties, said to Jones under his breath, 'My, but you're a wonder, sir!'

◇ ◇ ◇

On 17 March 1902 unto the world of golf Robert Tyre Jones Jnr was given. From an early age and until he retired from competitive golf at the age of 28, he gave and gave to the world of golf until he could give no more.

There are sufficient accounts of his early life to preclude the need for yet another here, but there are some happenings and influences that should be mentioned because of the part they played in producing this unique golfer. During his playing career he indicated his perception that predestination was applied to many events. Perhaps it was preordained that personalities and events should combine to create the setting in which his talents could develop and flourish.

Bobby's middle name 'Tyre', with its Old Testament and other overtones, was first given to Bobby's grandfather, Robert Tyre Jones. Born in 1849, here was a man, generally known as 'R.T.', with a considerable physical presence. He was 6′ 5″ tall, for that time a remarkable height. He had known hard times in the aftermath of the American Civil War, trying to help on his father's farm and in his cousin's general store in Northern Georgia. Believing that the nearby town of Canton could support a general store of its own, he committed his entire savings of $500 to the process of creating one. From that successful beginning, he was involved in the setting up of the Bank of Canton and then created the Canton Textile Mills that were to make his fortune. A man of strong faith, he served for forty years as Superintendent of the First Baptist Church in Canton and shunned 'womanising, smoking, cursing or drinking.'

Bobby's father was given the forenames of Robert Permedus and subsequently became widely known as 'The Colonel'. He was a more than useful baseball player and were it not for his own austere father, he would have signed a contract to play for the Brooklyn Club in the National League. A parental veto came into effect with the words, 'I didn't send you to college to become a professional baseball player' and instead a career was forged in the law. When R.T. was told that his son was a good baseball player, his retort was that 'You could not pay him a poorer compliment.' R.T. never saw his son play baseball.

R.T. carried his views on sport on to the next generation until he softened in later life. When playing in the 1922 US Amateur, Bobby received a telegram from his grandfather which said, 'Keep your ball in the fairway and make all the putts go down.' This glimmer of support revealed a major shift in attitude and had a considerable emotional impact on the young golfer. Disapproving strongly of playing any sport on the Sabbath, he eventually said to Bobby, 'If you must play on a Sunday, play well.' When Bobby returned to New York after his win in the 1926 British Open, he was met by his young wife Mary and his parents. Also there was R.T., who was at pains to point out to the press that he happened to be in New York on business and while there dropped down to see what was taking place. No one was duped.

In 1927, well-intentioned members of Atlanta Athletic Club raised $50,000 and gave it to Jones at a celebratory dinner to allow him to purchase his own house. After first accepting it, Jones felt it might threaten his amateur status and put out feelers to the United States Golf Association (USGA). Their response was that it might well warrant examination. A nod was as good as a wink and he returned the cheque. His short-term despondency at no longer being able to set up his own home evaporated when R.T. lent his grandson the exact amount. His austere side had not completely gone as he laid down strict terms: there was to be repayment – but only at the rate of $1 per year!

Perhaps it was inevitable that the Colonel was the opposite of his father. He saw life as something to be enjoyed rather than endured. Away from parental awareness he cursed, drank and told adult jokes. He took into adult life a resolve that his offspring would never be denied the opportunity to develop whatever sporting aptitude they might have.

The Colonel's wife, Clara Thomas, was short and slightly built, but not lacking in character. Calamity struck when their firstborn William Bailey Jones struggled in his early life with protracted vomiting and weight loss. He died when aged three months and Clara bemoaned the poor medical care provided in the small town of Canton. The cause of William's vomiting may well have been a condition called pyloric stenosis. If so, her views were valid as that condition would have been curable by a small operation. When she became pregnant again, she urged her husband to move to Atlanta to find better medical cover. Perhaps to get away from the oppressive influence of R.T., he needed little urging.

Soon after reaching Atlanta, the Colonel began work for the expanding Coca-Cola Company. As well as lamenting the sporting opportunities he was denied, he was always disappointed that he had not been given his father's middle name. Clara fell pregnant again and this child was named Robert Tyre after his grandfather.

Weighing only five pounds at birth, the newborn gave his parents continuing concern with a 'delicate stomach'. He was taken to a variety of doctors but apart from suggesting a diet of egg whites, pabulum and black-eyed peas they had no useful suggestions. By the time he was six he was described as 'an almost shockingly spindling youngster with an oversize head and legs with staring knees. Few youngsters at the romper age have less resembled, without being actually malformed, a future athletic champion.'

It was to address this worrying equation that the Colonel took his family to East Lake Golf Club, Atlanta for the summer and gave the boy his first exposure to golf. Though he never had a formal lesson, Bobby just watched the balanced rhythmical swing of the Scottish club professional Stewart 'Kiltie' Maiden who had been brought over from Carnoustie. He was also fortunate to find himself playing with two other talented youngsters, Perry Adair and Alexa Stirling. Within a few years Bobby's natural propensity to imitate produced a latent talent that was to flower over the decades that followed. He was greatly helped by his innate ability to mimic swings he watched. When friends of his father were at the house, he was often called upon to imitate various adults. Jones recalled that Judge Broyles never seemed to get as much fun out of the rendition of his own foibles as did the others present. Copying Maiden's flowing swing was a more fruitful strategy. By the time he reached his early teens it was clear that here was an exceptional talent.

During the First World War Bobby played in many exhibition matches, raising considerable sums for the war effort. The first series of matches were with his friends from Atlanta: Perry Adair, Alexa Stirling and Elaine Rosenthal. Golf for the four youngsters was simply fun and to be enjoyed. Subsequently, Chick Evans who as an amateur had won the US Open and the US Amateur in the same year in 1916, invited the sixteen-year-old Jones to partner him in a series of matches against leading professionals, further helping the relief funds.

Not only was he a golfing prodigy, Jones's educational achievements were sustained and considerable. In his later teens he entered Georgia Tech to study mechanical engineering. At first glance this might be seen as an unexpected choice of college and course, but Perry Adair being there may have been a factor. Although there was no family pattern of studying engineering, the subject may well have appealed to Jones's enquiring mind. Beyond engineering, the course included mathematics, geology, physics, chemistry and drawing. He completed his four-year course, finishing in the top third of his year, scoring marks in the 90s in English, maths and geology and in the 80s in chemistry, electrical engineering and physics.

Having graduated as a Bachelor of Science in Mechanical Engineering, he resolved to apply himself to the humanities and enrolled at Harvard to study English. He marked his arrival by setting a new record for the golf course at the Charles River Country Club. Having played college golf for Georgia Tech, he was ineligible to play for Harvard, but cheerfully took on the post of manager and coach. As he himself said, 'How else was I going to get the Crimson "H"?' He applied himself diligently to his studies, recalling spending all his surplus allowance in the bookstores 'around Scolley Square or, when I was a little better heeled, in Lauriat's basement.'

While there his golfing opportunities were stifled and it has been suggested that he applied for leave to play in the 1923 British Amateur, but permission was denied as it would have conflicted with his exam schedule. Even with minimal exposure, his level of play was maintained. On one occasion he played against the best ball of the entire six-man Harvard team and won. He pursued his studies on an accelerated timetable, with course work in German, French and British history. Happenings in Continental Europe 1817–1871 had to be tackled, as did Roman history. His classes encompassed the writings of Dryden, Shakespeare and Swift and aspects of Comparative Literature and Composition. He emerged with his valued Bachelor in Arts in English Literature.

Jones then spent a rather unsettled time in the real estate business, again perhaps as a means of keeping in touch with Perry Adair. During the summer of 1926, Jones had a realistic chance of winning the British Amateur until, afflicted by an acute neck spasm, he lost in the sixth round. He then won the British Open and US Open and only lost in the final of the US Amateur to George Von Elm, who had finished third in the British Open a few weeks earlier. His achievements in that year were only a little way behind those of the 1930 Grand Slam. Sensing that real estate was not for him, he enrolled in the autumn of 1926 in the Emory law school. His original plan was to complete the three-year course and he applied himself well to his studies, being placed second out of the 25 students after the first year.

His instructor in contracts, Professor Quillian, considered Jones to have 'one of the finest legal minds of any student I've ever known.' Towards the end of the autumn term of 1927, he entered himself for the Georgia bar examination to provide himself with a measure of his progress. Perhaps a little to his own surprise, he passed and as this entitled him to take up the law immediately, he was able to pass up on the option of completing the rest of the course at Emory.

Of more interest than his ability to satisfy examiners was the breadth and depth of his intellect and the enquiring nature of his mind. He loved opera, for example; and while travelling to the first Walker Cup at the National Golf Links on Long Island, his reading material on the train was Cicero's *Orations Against Cataline*. Vexed at his tendency to deprecate his golfing ability, Jones once said, 'this bird Cicero was a long way from hating himself. I wish I could think as much of my golf as he did of his statesmanship. I might do better in these blamed tournaments.' Sports writer Grantland Rice pointed out how 'in starting out for a Championship, [Jones] might be found with a Latin book or a calculus treatise, with all thought of golf eliminated until he reached the field of battle.' At other times he would be found discussing Einstein and the fourth dimension. His practice for the 1923 US Amateur at Flossmoor was wretched, so his strategy between the two qualifying rounds on the Saturday and the Monday was to stay in his bed in the hotel on the Sunday, reading Papini's *Life of Christ*.

Jones's own writings revealed the rich vein of thinking from which he drew his text. He did however admit that the creation of written work did not come easily. Corresponding with golf writer Pat Ward-Thomas he revealed, 'I am not one of those fortunate persons who can sit down before a typewriter and spill out words that make sense. The act of creation on a blank page costs me no end of pain.'

Broadcaster Alistair Cooke, in a review he entitled 'The Missing Aristotle Papers' on the instructional articles that made up *Bobby Jones on Golf*, revealed his admiration for the quality of Jones's writing. He wrote:

> Jones's gift for distilling a complex emotion into the barest language would not have shamed John Donne; his

meticulous insistence on the right word to impress the
right visual image was worthy of fussy old Flaubert; and
his unique personal gift was to take apart many of the club
clichés with a touch of grim Lippmannesque humour.

Fuelled by his genuine modesty, Jones wrote back to
Cooke with the tongue-in-cheek comment, 'Offhand, I
can't think of another contemporary author who has been
compared in one piece to Aristotle, Flaubert, John Donne
and Walter Lippmann.'

Looking back, his grandson recalled how Jones would
'go out on a fishing boat with his friend, Charlie Elliott, the
editor of *Outdoor Life* and for hours they would talk about
syntax, sometimes English, sometimes Latin.' However it
should not be deduced from the foregoing that Jones was
too serious about life or himself. Charles Price points out
that 'He was not the least bit calculating or priggish. He
smoked to excess on the course, drank corn whisky off it,
swore magnificently in either place, and could listen to, or
tell, an off-color story in the locker-room afterward. He was
spontaneous, affectionate, and loyal to his friends, all of
whom called him Bob.'

The remaining piece of the jigsaw that allowed his
genius to find its full expression was Oscar Bane 'Pop'
Keeler. Originally a journalist, he not only became Jones's
mouthpiece to the world at large but more crucially a source
of wise counsel and a steadying influence. During the early
years, repeated disappointments threatened to weaken the
young golfer's resolve and it took all of Keeler's guile to keep
young Bobby's spirits up.

During the period of his playing career when he won championship after championship, Jones was shielded by Keeler from the Press. The reporters got their material from the mouth of Keeler, an arrangement which in many ways suited them as their work was already half done. What is more important, Jones was spared the exhausting process of being interrogated and the unsettling experience of being asked to analyse what he was doing to achieve his successes.

Keeler was also an intellectual stimulus to Jones as they travelled and roomed together. Best viewed as a benevolent uncle, O.B. brought the best out of his young ward and made long train journeys pass quickly. It is probably true to say that without Keeler the playing record of Jones would have been diminished.

CHAPTER TWO

On genius and temperament

'Talent hits a target no one else can hit:
genius hits a target no one else can see.'

ARTHUR SCHOPENHAUER

Bobby Jones was a genius at golf.

At first glance it might appear to be a little over the top to suggest this. However, not only does the contention warrant serious consideration, it deserves acceptance. Such a suggestion has been made at least twice before. The first located reference is the *New York Times* issue of 26 June 1926 which, quoting from the correspondent of the *Observer*, stated:

> There is no parallel in the history of golf, and I do not suppose there ever will be again. Mr Bobby Jones is just a genius, and they are not born every day.

The second is by golf writer Charles Price, who revered Jones as a golfer and as a man. He wrote:

The explanation for Bobby Jones's astounding golf is quite simple. He had a genius for the game.

It is possible to be a genius as an adult after an unremarkable childhood and it is equally possible to be a child prodigy and thereafter mundane in later life, on occasions after a spectacular burnout. There is also a cohort of individuals who are both child prodigies in their earliest years and geniuses as an adult, the former phase flowing irresistibly into the latter. Jones was such an individual.

In a child prodigy, one sees someone who at a very early age masters a difficult skill to the level of an adult. At the age of five Mozart was composing minuets. Aged six he was performing in concerts on harpsichord and violin. By nine he had composed his first symphony and at the age of twelve his first opera. By the time Prokofiev entered the St Petersburg conservatory at the age of thirteen, he had a portfolio of four operas, two sonatas and some piano pieces. William Rowan Hamilton, later a leading mathematician, read Hebrew by the age of seven and by the age of twelve had studied Arabic, Persian, Greek, Latin, Syriac, Sanskrit and four other foreign languages.

A child prodigy displays one key feature of genius that was stressed by Immanuel Kant: the ability to independently arrive at and understand concepts that would normally have to be taught by an adult. This is how Jones came to golf – without lessons and simply by grafting his own perception of the essence of golf onto what he saw East Lake's Stewart Maiden do. This aspect sets him apart from every other golfer before or since. From his play in his early years,

Jones was clearly a child prodigy, not just from his play and achievements, but also from the way he acquired a game and swing that was all his own.

He had little time for practice as a discipline, though he would go on to the practice ground on occasion if he felt a particular matter needed to be addressed. Having done so to his satisfaction, he would then leave. His golf was instinctive and intuitive. He spent only three months in each year in what might be considered competitive golf. During the part of his golfing career referred to by Keeler as the 'seven fat years' from 1923 to 1930, he only played in five tournaments other than the Majors – and won four of them! In the cauldron of the fiercest competition, from standing up to the ball to hitting his shot was timed at three seconds. This is to be contrasted with the laboured mechanics of the players of today.

In the period that Keeler described as the 'seven lean years' between 1916 and 1923, Jones underwent a gradual evolution from child prodigy into the genius he was later able to express in the seven fat years. To paraphrase Owen Meredith, Earl of Lytton, talent does what it can, but genius does what it must. Jones knew that he had to scale heights beyond the reach of others. However, in the early lean years he had a real problem that prevented this genius from being expressed – the destructive effect of his own temperament. Because of its relevance to his subsequent development in the run up to the British Open at Royal Lytham & St Anne's, this problem merits further examination. The few reported instances of ill temper are inevitably just a small fragment of what must have been a consistent aspect of his golfing excursions.

Some have suggested that the problems experienced by the young Jones were simply those of a hot-headed youth who was taking his time to find his equilibrium, but clearly they were based on something much deeper than that. In his earliest days on the makeshift two-hole 'course' near the house he stayed in at East Lake, he would at times dance with rage in the middle of the road if a shot failed to meet his expectations. And this was at the age of six.

The inner force that created Jones's instinctive ability also created a furious and destructive energy within. One of the other youngsters with whom he played was the exceptionally talented Alexa Stirling. She later recalled:

> Let him make one poor shot and he'd turn livid with rage, throw his club after the ball, or break it over his knee, or kick at the ground and let out a stream of very adult oaths. As I grew into my teens, Bob's temper tantrums began to embarrass me. It was perhaps amusing to see an eight-year-old break his club when he made a bad shot, but not so amusing when he was twelve or thirteen.

Bobby may have learnt colourful language from the adults with whom he played, but he had little control over himself and his ability to suppress such expressions when he knew he ought to. On another occasion Alexa, playing with her father, came across Jones who had just played a bad shot. He threw his club and swore aloud. This greatly offended Alexa's father who said to Jones, 'Young man, don't you know better than to use language like that in front of a lady?' Alexa described how her father 'took me by the hand and marched me off the course.' She was not allowed to play with Jones for two years.

In 1915 Grantland Rice watched the thirteen-year-old Jones in the company of Alex Smith and Long Jim Barnes, both of whom subsequently won the US Open. After Jones 'violently repositioned' his club in his bag after a shot that did not meet expectations, Smith concluded, 'It's a shame but he'll never make a golfer – too much temper.' Barnes could see beyond the inner rage and disagreed: 'This kid will be one of the greatest in a few more years,' he predicted. Rice added, 'He isn't just satisfied with a good shot. He wants it to be perfect – stone dead. But you're correct about that temper, Alex. He's a fighting cock – a hothead. If he can't learn to control it, he'll never play the kind of golf he's capable of shooting.'

In 1916 Jones was taken with Perry Adair by Perry's father to play in the US Amateur Championship at Merion Cricket Club, Philadelphia. Aged only fourteen, he was the subject of much interest, more so after his 74 in the first round of the qualifying stages. In the first round of match play, he gave a glimpse of his youthful innocence, as he offered his opponent chewing gum as they left the first tee. He was playing against Eben Byers, who had been US Amateur Champion in 1906 and was by then aged 39. Byers also had a short fuse and the proffered chewing gum was brusquely declined. Both players expressed their unhappiness at poor shots by throwing clubs; players in the following match felt they were watching jugglers. At the twelfth hole, Byers threw a club out of bounds and would not let his caddie retrieve it. Jones, as guilty as Byers of club throwing, later commented wryly that 'I think the main reason I beat him was that he ran out of clubs first.'

Club throwing does appear to have been a more widespread happening then than now. Jones was playing an exhibition match with Perry Adair against George Simpson and Alex Cunningham. George was teasing Alex about his poor play and when he missed an eighteen-inch putt at the fifteenth hole it was just too much for Alex. Jones describes how Alex 'threw his putter at least a hundred yards into some trees. It was the longest club throw I had ever seen.'

Early in 1918, Jones was in Canada, playing against Jerry Travers in one of a series of exhibition matches that raised money for the war effort. On the very first green, Jones missed a short putt and became so enraged that he hurled his club far over the heads of the crowds into the trees and undergrowth surrounding the course. The Canadian gallery laughed at this outburst and joined in the search for the putter that had disappeared into the woods.

Later that year, Alexa Stirling had won the first of what would turn out to be three consecutive US Women's Amateur Championships. She was by then once more playing with Jones, partnering him against Perry Adair and Elaine Rosenthal in exhibition matches. In one match Jones was playing badly, taking 87 shots for his round. He and Alexa lost 5 & 3. When he missed an easy shot at the eighth, she described how 'I saw the blood climb his neck and flood his face. Then he picked up his ball, took a full pitcher's wind up and threw his ball into the woods. A gasp of surprise and shock went through the large crowd watching us. I wished the ground would open up and let me sink from sight.'

When she later chastised him for his actions, his response was, 'I don't give a damn what anyone thinks of me. I only get mad at myself.' It was said that in these war relief matches Jones gave a mixture of sensational golf and volatile temper tantrums. Grantland Rice perceptively commented that Jones was 'a short rotund kid with the face of an angel and temper of a timberwolf.' On another occasion he expressed his concern that 'That one fault could prove to be his greatest hazard.'

In the 1919 US Amateur at Oakmont, Jones was still struggling against the rage that burnt within. When playing against W.C. Fownes Jnr, Jones was barely in control of himself, though he did defeat the former champion 5 & 3. One sports writer noted that Jones experienced 'smouldering wrath' and 'supreme disgust' at his own errors.

Bobby nevertheless reached the final, in which his opponent was local favourite S. Davidson Herron. It was forecast that if Herron established an early lead, Jones might struggle to contain his temper. All square after eighteen holes, Jones found himself two down nine holes later and his mood was not helped by the partisan crowd cheering when he failed to get out of a bunker. The 30th hole saw the critical incident. Marshals used megaphones to control spectators and as Jones started his backswing with his brassie, 'a horn-rimmed bespectacled official saw a boy 400 yards away move two inches and bellowed "Fore!" into his megaphone.' Unsurprisingly, Jones barely made contact with his ball, which trickled into a nearby bunker. An incandescent Jones failed to get out in two further shots and angrily plucked the ball off the sand, conceding the hole. He lost the next hole and the match was quickly over.

The following year the US Amateur was held at the Engineers' Country Club on Long Island and there was continuing evidence of the frailty of Jones's temperament. In the third round, 'when his drives began swerving and his irons temporarily refused to rescue him, his face became flushed with anger, [but] when he got away a screaming drive on the long twelfth that travelled 320 yards and came to rest in the mathematical centre of the fairway, his good spirits returned to him.'

In the semi-final against Francis Ouimet, Jones found himself two down playing the seventeenth hole in the morning round. After over-hitting a bunker shot he 'socked his club back into his bag with a vicious movement.' After missing a 'teeny little putkkpoo' on the eighteenth to fall three down, he picked up his ball and drop-kicked it into the rough. A sports writer summed up the play of Jones at Brae Burn on another occasion by saying, 'Some interesting golf was shown during the match, interspersed with some pranks by Jones which will have to be corrected if this player expects to rank with the best in the country. Although Jones is only a boy, his display of temper when things went wrong did not appeal to the gallery.'

Long Jim Barnes put things in perspective after watching Jones play in the 1921 US Open and saw a good future for the fiery Georgian: 'Never mind that club throwing and the beatings he's taking. Defeat will make him great. He's not satisfied now with a pretty good shot. He has to be perfect. That's the way a good artist must feel.'

In the first and second rounds of the 1921 British Open at St Andrews, Jones was paired with the eventual winner

Jock Hutchison. The two got on well and subsequently became good friends. After Jones retired, Hutchison was invited for many years to play in the Masters and with Fred McLeod became the honorary starter in 1963. Back in 1921, Hutchison saw Jones's temper flare on the sixteenth green when after missing a three-foot putt he tossed his putter to the ground and began to leave the green. The older man caught up with the younger and gave him a severe reprimand for his conduct. Jones later recalled this lecture as a telling factor in his subsequent quelling of his outbursts.

Some writers have given weight to the consequences of a minor event that occurred in 1921. Leaving the seventeenth green during the US Amateur after missing a putt, Jones lightly tossed his putter without petulance or malice towards his bag. It ricocheted off the bag and made glancing contact with a lady spectator. In several subsequent accounts, which only started emerging many years later, it is suggested that George Walker, President of the USGA, wrote to Jones reporting that the lady had made a complaint and that unless he improved his problems with his temper he would never be allowed to play in USGA events. It is further stated that Jones sent a contrite reply. There must be some doubts about this matter. George Walker was not President of the USGA at the time. There is no copy of any letter from the USGA to Jones nor of any reply from him, nor any mention of the matter in the USGA files.

While others viewed his tantrums with displeasure, the great golf writer Bernard Darwin, whose own temperament on the course was fragile at times, took a slightly more sanguine approach. Looking back in the 1930s, he mused how 'the matter of losing the temper hardly plays, I think, the part in golf that it once did.' Darwin went on:

> Where are the truly great losers of their temper? Their fires are now with the snows of yesterday. The man who prayed to heaven to consume the links; the man who threw his clubs into the sea and was then nearly drowned in rescuing them; the man who laid his bag on the railway line and saw the contents reduced to spillikins – these are now hacking furious divots out of asphodel and have not left their peers.

Reflecting on the 1914 match between Jones and Byers mentioned earlier, Darwin wrote:

> That was a noteworthy beginning, and Bobby might have become the supreme club-thrower as well as the supreme golfer. Alas, he gave it all up and became outwardly at least a man of ice, so that this relief for our pent-up feelings is no longer permissible.

By the early 1920s, Jones was realising that not only were his temper outbursts embarrassing and unacceptable to others, but more importantly they were holding him back from fulfilling his potential and ultimately his destiny. He resolved somehow to bring about a transformation that would quell his temper, but the outcome was that it would be replaced with an inward burning flame that would threaten to consume him. Anticipating the changes he would have to make he commented that 'Golf may be a sophisticated game. At least it is usually played with the outward appearance of great dignity. It is nevertheless a game of considerable passion, either of the explosive type or that which burns inwardly and sears the soul.' In the spring of 1930 he admitted, 'I've never got rid of my temper. I still get as mad as blazes, but I don't show it; I suppress it.' A close friend, Harrison Johnston, who won the US Amateur in 1929 had a great insight into the equation: 'These outbursts of temper were safety valves for his nervous system. As he grew older and saw how undignified it looked to give way to his feelings, Bobby smothered them – and in doing so generated a human volcano beneath the surface.'

CHAPTER THREE

The first crossing

Bobby Jones's trip across the Atlantic in 1926 was his second such journey, the first having been five years earlier. As a prelude to the Open at St Anne's, an examination of the 1921 trip provides a useful insight into his earlier experiences of links golf. It also offers a perception of how, five years later, he would have approached his second foray into what would still have been a challenging undertaking.

For a nineteen-year-old Jones, the feelings generated by an Atlantic crossing in 1921 must have been complex. Buoyed by the innocence of youth, there would have been excitement, curiosity and exhilaration. These sensations however would have been tempered by concern about the unknown and about whether the intimidating aspects of British society, so much at odds with life in the Southern states of America, would have an inhibiting effect.

Although without the stabilising influence of his father, he would nonetheless have been well cushioned by others in the American expeditionary golfing team. Bobby was in awe of

Francis Ouimet who at the same age had won the US Open at Brookline, beating Harry Vardon and Ted Ray in an epic play-off. To Jones, Ouimet was an arm around the shoulders and a source of inspiration and security. At this stage of their lives, Jones and Chick Evans were good friends and keen rivals. In later years, Evans, fuming about the extent to which his own achievements had been rendered insignificant by what Jones accomplished, was to harbour disappointing resentment against the Georgian. The others in the American party made up a cohesive team, eager firstly to take on the cream of the British golfers on their own patch in an informal forerunner to what would become the Walker Cup, and secondly to produce an American winner of the British Amateur Championship. Both events were to be played over the links of the Royal Liverpool Golf Club, at Hoylake.

In *Down the Fairway*, Jones prefaces his own account of the trip by summarising it thus:

> I went to Great Britain in 1921 and added a lot to my meagre stock of golfing education by taking a lacing in the British amateur championship at Hoylake and performing one last superbly childish gesture by picking up – that is, withdrawing – in the British Open championship at St Andrews.

The course at Hoylake must have come as a shock to the youthful Jones. Hard burnt fairways along which drives would run forever. Almost but not quite flat yet slick greens that could play havoc with the confidence needed for good putting. His opponents were different to those he had come up against before – strange accents, distant attitudes. The crowds were made up of drably attired individuals who remained silent whether the shot was good or bad. Jones's own summary was that he 'learned quite a bit at Hoylake, which was well dried out with the hard turf and the greens like glass; they don't water the greens over there; they believe in letting nature taking its course with golf. And I don't know but they're right.' Later in life, writing to Pat Ward-Thomas, Jones pointed out:

> Although I did not feel this way in the beginning, I am happy now that I did not miss playing seaside golf when the greens were hard and unwatered and the fairways and putting surfaces like glass. Nothing resulting from man-made design can equal the testing qualities of such conditions.

In *The Boys' Life of Bobby Jones*, Keeler describes how Jones approached his first Atlantic crossing:

> By the next spring he was in a happy and excited frame of mind, setting sail for Britain with a jolly party of American amateurs, to play in the British Amateur championship at old Hoylake, and – Bobby, at any rate – in the British Open at St Andrews. It was the first really organised invasion of the British championship by American amateurs, and the informal team match played before the tournament, and won by the Americans, was the forerunner of the Walker Cup international match now played biennially, in alternate countries.

When he came to Hoylake he learned that one must have a variety of golf, to cope with the British conditions; the sweeping sea-breeze bothered him no end; his beautiful, steep pitch shots bounded from the baked putting surfaces as if from cement; and he had not acquired the deft and useful run-up approach that is a necessity in dry and windy weather ... The visitors were so dismayed by the greens that, as a concession, several buckets were poured about the pin on one of the driest surfaces, so that a ball might be eased up and stopped somewhere near the hole – until the water was absorbed.

The informal match was the outcome of the initiative of George Herbert Walker. The *New York Times* of 8 January 1921 had announced that he had donated the 'Walker Cup' for an international event. Some suggested this might encourage the USGA to cover the costs of the trip, but they did not pay the team's expenses. Having being given special permission to finish his junior year at Georgia Tech early, Jones sailed with Ouimet and the captain, William Fownes, on the *Caronia* on 30 April, reaching Liverpool on 9 May. Ouimet introduced Jones to the awaiting reporters as 'our baby'. Primed by Harry Vardon's report on his ability, the journalists were impressed by Jones, who smiled and smoked a large cigar! The press concluded that he had 'the most loveable manner and engaging smile.'

The indications are that overall Jones adapted reasonably well to Britain. It was not until 1923 that his problems with temperament were overcome, so at this time he could still be volatile. In the international match between Great Britain and the United States that was played on 21 May 1921, all went well as Jones partnered Chick Evans in the first foursomes. The golf they produced was exceptional. The *New York Times* described them as 'irresistible as a foursome combination. They won hole after hole, until at the eighth green they were in the commanding position of being 6 up.'

The *Star* reported that 'Jones hit the first ball and he and Evans proceeded to dissipate the idea that Americans were only four-ball and not foursome players, doing the first five holes in 4, 4, 4, 2 and 4, which represents unbeatable golf.' The outcome of the afternoon singles gives an indication of the relative contribution of each American in the morning match, as Evans lost to Cyril Tolley 4 & 3, while Jones saw off R.H. de Montmorency by the same margin. The *New York Times* commented that 'Jones, playing with a steadiness which excited admiration, was never seriously troubled.' Associated Press concluded that 'Jones, through his spectacular driving and accurate putting, today appears to the British as a formidable entry for the Championship.'

After the first round in the Amateur, an event based on eighteen-hole matches until the final, which was played over 36 holes, this view had become even more firmly held. For those interested in a wager, odds at the time for a Jones win were 5/1, for Ouimet 6/1, for Evans 7/1 and for the redoubtable English golfer Tolley 10/1.

The American reader was able to follow the event as it was featured on the front page of the *New York Times*, perhaps reflecting the interest generated by Jones playing. The young Georgian had the unnerving privilege of being in the first match and playing the first shot. Avoiding the internal out of bounds, he opened with a birdie three and beat his opponent G.C. Manford by 3 & 2.

While all went well for the Americans on the first day, the second day saw the unexpected exit of both Ouimet and Evans. Jones survived the second round but only in an extraordinary match. The *New York Times* dealt with the quality of play gently:

Jones displayed a curious reversal of form in his second round match with a practically unknown player E.A. Hamlet who learnt his golf on the nine hole chicken run at Wrexham and whose outfit comprises eight clubs.

Jones was completely off his game. He took 85 for the round and pulled his match out of the fire with difficulty on the last green. Hamlet was going steadily along on the outward journey and Jones became annoyed at his own indifferent display. At the fifth hole, when he drove into a bush and played a left handed shot into a different bush, he vented his chagrin by kicking at the bush. At another hole, on missing a short putt, he dashed his putter to the ground. Altogether he could not plume himself on this display. He was 1 down at the fifth, 2 down at the seventh and remained 2 down until the fifteenth where Hamlet, who should have finished the match there, developed nervousness and lost the hole. Though 2 down [*sic*] with 3 to go, Jones roused himself and took the holes, thereby surviving the second round. Two thousand people saw him finish and cheered his successful effort to pull himself out of the fire.

The Times of London was more frank:

Jones made an amazing display of bad golf for a man of his parts. It seems churlish not to praise Hamlet for so nearly extinguishing the great American, but the truth compels the admission that Hamlet is not a good player. It was entirely the ludicrous play of Jones that made any kind of match of it. It was really dreadful: the crowd did not know whether to laugh or cry.

Hamlet was a florist by trade and an 'obscure amateur' with what journalist George Greenwood described as 'a ridiculous style'. There was for some time a real prospect that Hamlet would win. 'It really seemed as if he were going to beat Bobby, which, as Euclid would have remarked, would have been absurd,' wrote Bernard Darwin. 'It was a farcical affair and the crowd were divided between patriotism, fury and laughter.' Darwin was not only reporting but also competing, making his way to the sixth round where he put out the last American Fred Wright, before losing in the quarter-final to the eventual winner, Willie Hunter.

Jones took a pragmatic view of his first- and second-round matches:

I played the quaintest golf all through Britain; good and bad and terrible golf. In my first match in the

championship I played well and beat a chap named
Manford with a card of about par. Then I met a Mr.
Hamlet, who shot an 87, and I was just good enough to
beat him 1 up. I had to win the last two holes to do it,
and he assisted me ably by missing a four-foot putt at the
seventeenth, while my uncertain putt at the last green,
half-stymied by his previous stroke, hit his ball at the edge
of the cup, and mine dropped in and his stayed out. That
was plain luck.

He steadied up in the afternoon round, beating Robert
Harris 6 & 5, but was still not on his game. The *New York
Times* noted that 'Jones was not extended in his third
round engagement with Harris, the 1914 finalist. This was
fortunate, as Bobby himself was playing rather poorly.' The
report went on to say:

> It is rather difficult to account for Jones falling away
> from grace, and it is the opinion here that his form as
> shown today will not carry him through. Putting was
> his weakest feature. He was 3 up at the turn and having
> nothing to beat, he easily brought a disappointing
> match to a finish on the fourteenth green [*sic*], 6 up
> and five to play.

This prediction came to fruition the next day when Jones
was badly defeated by his opponent Allan Graham. The earlier
optimistic coverage from the *New York Times* was replaced
by subdued reporting of a grim day for the remaining
American players:

It was another day of slaughter of favourites in the play for the British Amateur golf championship today. 'Bobby' Jones had shaken the faith of his admirers by his indifferent play yesterday and consequently there was no great surprise when he was beaten by Allan Graham, brother of the famous John (Jack) Graham, one of the most finished golfers who has ever lived. Jones was still below form. He would have needed to have been at his best to get the better of Graham, but he was not, and he met with rather a bad beating. His huge drives made Graham always play the odd, but near the greens the Hoylake man outplayed his rival, and when the game finished on the thirteenth green, he had five 3's on his card. 'Bobby' had no luck, as he was in bunkers at the fourth and sixth and at the foot of a wooden fence at the eighth. The latter difficulty he surmounted in novel fashion. It was impossible to play out, so he banged the ball against the fence with the iron and it rebounded onto the green forty yards away. Yet he lost the hole, missing a two foot putt for a half.

He was 4 down at the sixth, registered his only win at the seventh and dropped steadily back, until beaten, 6 up and 5 to play. Graham's putting was extraordinary. Four yard putts presented no difficulty and he holed a ten yarder for a 3 at the 380 yard ninth hole.

Graham 543-345-463=37
Jones 645-446-364=42

Graham 435-4 16
Jones 545-4 18

Jones said after the match that his defeat was merely due to his own bad play. 'When you meet a man playing well and you are playing badly, why you're just out of luck,' he remarked.

In *The Times* of London, Darwin reported:

> The passing of Tolley, however, was as nothing compared with the swamping of Jones by Graham. Jones was off his game. Great player as he is, he does not possess the temperament to bullock his way through a British Amateur Championship.

There is no doubt that Graham was an accomplished player in his own right, though some in the press sought to make light of his ability. It was noted that he had borrowed three clubs from his sister to make up a set, including a brass putter of unusual appearance. Greenwood, writing in the *Daily Telegraph*, described him as tall and sleepy looking, and appearing to be bored with the game, sauntering around the course:

> As he came across his ball, you could almost hear him say 'Oh confound it, here is another one of those beastly golf balls. I suppose I must hit it.' He declined to wear spiked shoes that might stop him slipping on the greens on the grounds that they were a nuisance around the house. Whatever his eccentricities, he beat an off-form Jones comprehensively.

At this stage of his golfing career Jones was firmly stuck in what we have earlier seen Keeler describe as the seven lean years, which lasted until his first major win in the US Open at Inwood in 1923. His problems with temperament were unresolved and it must have become an increasingly real concern to him, as it was to others, that he was never going to become a winner of the events that really mattered. He had to suppress the creeping self-doubt in his own ability but inevitably this dimension must have fuelled his difficulties with temperament. Chastened and unsettled, he headed north to the British Open at St Andrews.

If, at Hoylake, Jones's experiences lurched from farcical comedy to considerable disappointment, his experience at the British Open at St Andrews was to be simple dark tragedy. Paraphrasing Winston Churchill's thoughts about Russia, Jones was to discover that the Old Course was a riddle, wrapped in a mystery inside an enigma. She was in no mood to reveal her intrigue and charm to the youngster on first acquaintance.

Keeler later summed up the matter in characteristic style:

If, as the great and wise M. Maeterlinck has suggested, the present and the future really are co-existent, Bobby Jones should have stepped out reverently upon the silken turf of the most famous course in the world. He should have loved it at once – for he was to love it beyond all other courses. And certainly he should never have behaved as he did in the British open of 1921; for there, in the future, superimposed on the smooth pastel of the eighteenth green is the same Bobby Jones carried high on broad Scottish shoulders above a gallery of cheering, scrambling thousands –

winner of the British Open championship with the lowest score yet recorded.

However, in 1921 Jones had no immediate affection for the Old Course. To some extent he overcame this reaction by recovering from a modest opening round of 78 with a second round of 74, leaving him just five shots behind the leader, Jock Hutchison. Jones played with Hutchison, the eventual winner, in the first two rounds and witnessed his hole-in-one at the eighth. At the next hole, Hutchison smacked a huge drive that drew on the breeze not only to reach the green – a wallop of some 303 yards – but to roll up to the hole and actually touch the rim. Tommy Kerrigan, who was on the green at the time, said the ball really ought to have dropped, but instead of going 1-1 Hutchison had to settle for 1-2 – four under par for the two holes!

Next morning, Jones struggled over the first nine holes of the third round. Unable to master the intriguing contours of the ancient links, he needed either 43 or 46 shots to get to the turn – accounts at the time, and since, differ. What is without doubt is that his famously short temper was now close to breaking. He took a six at the tenth and pulled his tee shot at the short eleventh into Hill bunker. Again there are various accounts of the fine detail of events. Some contend that he failed to get out of Hill, others that he did after several shots. It has been suggested that he then drove his ball far into the Eden estuary, but others indicate this did not happen. Some say he immediately tore his card up, others that he did not.

What is beyond doubt is that Jones did not complete the hole and did not return any score beyond the tenth –

instant disqualification. He continued to play in and later that day rather inexplicably went on to play his fourth round, returning a 72 that, of course, did not count.

Jones was remorseful then and remained so for the remainder of his life. Writing in 1927 he said:

> I have some sterling regrets in golf. This is the principal regret – that ever I quit in a competition. I know it's not regarded as reprehensible, in a medal-play against a field. I know some great players and fine sportsmen have done it, when they were simply going bad and had no chance for a good showing. But I was a youngster, still making my reputation. And I often have wished I could in some way offer a general apology for picking up my ball on the eleventh green of the third round, when I had a short putt left for a horrid 6. It means nothing to the world of golf. But it means something to me. Much more now that it did six years ago, when I took 46 for the first nine of the third round, and a 6 at the tenth and making a 6 at the eleventh, and said to myself, 'What's the use?'

Writing in 1929, Jones revealed his initial impression of the Old Course at St Andrews:

> When I first played there – in 1921 – I was unable to understand the reverence with which the place was regarded by our British friends. I considered St Andrews among the very worst golf courses I had ever seen, and I am afraid that I was even disrespectful of its difficulty.

The maddening part of the whole thing was that while I was certain that the course was easy, I simply could not make a good score.

Yet I did begin to think a little when a course so unprepossessing forced me to take forty-six to the turn in the third round of the tournament, and finally goaded me into the disgraceful act of picking up my ball after taking a pair of sixes at the tenth and eleventh holes. I must, however, give myself the credit to say that even then I was beginning to know St Andrews – at least to know that the Old Course was not to be taken lightly.

There is always a way at St Andrews, although it is not always the obvious way, and in trying to find it, there is more to be learned on this Scottish course than in playing a hundred ordinary American golf courses.

In 1958 Jones made a memorable speech when he accepted the Freedom of St Andrews, becoming after Benjamin Franklin the second American to do so. Referring back to 1921 he described how in the third round:

The wind was really blowing in my face. That day it was really blowing! I reached the turn in 43, and when I was playing the 7th, 8th and 9th, I thought, 'Well, that's fine. I'll be blowing home with the wind.' Well, as I stood on the 10th tee it turned right round and it blew home all the way against me. I got a 6 at the 10th, and then, at the 11th, I put my shot into Hill bunker, not Strath, as they said. They also say that when I got out of that bunker I hit my ball into the Eden. That's not so, for I never did get the ball out of Hill bunker.

In *Down the Fairway*, Jones indicates that he did not tear his card up but other accounts said that he had. Perhaps this is the only unclear aspect of the happening that subsequently became more defined when, in 1958, an article appeared in the *St Andrews Citizen* giving the clear recollection of an eye-witness. David Anderson, the owner of a hotel in St Andrews, saw Jones tear up his card on the twelfth hole, where there were no more than a dozen spectators:

It happened after Bobby had driven off the twelfth tee. Walking up the fairway, Bobby asked the marker for his card, [and] after a short scrutiny, cooly and deliberately tore it to shreds.

As Jones set sail back home, the impression he had made upon the British golfing public was summed up by the *Dundee Courier* which concluded that 'Master Bobbie Jones is a boy, and a rather ordinary boy, after all.' It was to Jones's credit that he was able to return to the United States in good spirits with, externally at least, no harm done after what must have been a chastening experience. Internally, his trip became one of a number of factors that helped him achieve the transformation from the seething youth often on the brink of explosion to the triumphant adult, who while winning time and again was at the same time draining himself from within.

CHAPTER FOUR

The transformation

As mentioned previously, Jones's biographer O.B. Keeler described Bobby's golf as occurring in two phases: the seven lean years from 1916 to 1923 and the seven fat years from 1923 to 1930. In drawing upon this biblical comparison, he was nearly entirely correct – however, the second element was actually eight years not seven! Even allowing for the fact that Jones was in the first period maturing as a person and as a golfer, the contrast between the two phases – explosive temperament as opposed to bottled-up strain – is as emphatic as it can be.

In the first phase, Jones won nothing of significance; in the second he won practically everything, but at an appalling internal cost. In between the two was a phase of transformation. Different writers have ascribed the transformation to a variety of factors and perhaps a valid conclusion is that it was due to a combination of them all.

At this time the British Amateur and the US Amateur were as important and as difficult to win as the British Open and the US Open. The calibre of the leading players who were likely to be in contention was even and comparable in the four events. For leading amateurs like Chick Evans, Francis Ouimet and Bobby Jones, these championships constituted the four Majors that needed to be won to secure a place in golfing history.

From 1916 to 1922 – the 'lean years' – Jones's record was as follows:

US Amateur

1916 at Merion Cricket Club, lost in the quarter-final to Robert Gardner 5 & 3

1919 at Oakmont Country Club, lost in the final to S. Davidson Herron 5 & 4

1920 at Engineers' Country Club, lost in the semi-final to Francis Ouimet 6 & 5

1921 at St Louis Country Club, lost in the quarter-final to Willie Hunter 2 & 1

1922 at The Country Club, Brookline, lost in the semi-final to Jess Sweetser 8 & 7

US Open

1920 at Inverness Club 78-74-70-77=299 finished tied 8th, four shots behind the winner Ted Ray

1921 at Columbia Country Club 78-71-77-77=303 finished 5th, fourteen shots behind the winner Jim Barnes

1922 at Skokie Country Club 74-72-70-73=289 finished 2nd, one shot behind the winner Gene Sarazen

British Amateur

1921 at Royal Liverpool Golf Club, Hoylake, lost in the fourth round to Allan Graham 6 & 5

British Open

1921 at the Old Course, St Andrews, failed to complete the eleventh hole in the third round

From 1923 to 1930 – the 'fat years' – Jones's record was as follows:

US Amateur

1923 at Flossmoor Country Club, lost in the second round to Max Marston 2 & 1
1924 at Merion Cricket Club, won the final defeating George Von Elm 9 & 8
1925 at Oakmont Country Club, won the final defeating Watts Gunn 8 & 7
1926 at Baltusrol Golf Club, lost in the final to George Von Elm 2 & 1
1927 at Minikahda Club, won the final defeating Chick Evans 8 & 7
1928 at Brae Burn Country Club, won the final defeating Philip Perkins 10 & 9
1929 at Pebble Beach Golf Links, lost in the first round to Johnny Goodman by 1 hole

1930 at Merion Cricket Club, won final defeating Eugene V. Homans 8 & 7

US Open

1923 at Inwood Country Club (71-73-76-76=296), finished tied 1st with Bobbie Cruickshank – won 76 to 78 in eighteen-hole play-off
1924 at Oakland Hills Country Club (74-73-75-78=300), finished 2nd, three strokes behind winner Cyril Walker
1925 at Worcester Country Club (77-70-70-74=291), finished tied 1st with Willie Macfarlane – lost 75-72=147 to 75-73=148 in 36-hole play-off
1926 at Scioto Country Club (70-79-71-73=293), won by one stroke from Willie Turnesa
1927 at Oakmont Country Club (76-77-79-77=309), finished tied 11th, eight strokes behind winner Tommy Armour
1928 at Olympia Fields Country Club (73-71-73-77=294), finished tied 1st with Johnny Farrell – lost 70-73=143 to 73-71=144 in 36-hole play-off
1929 at Winged Foot Golf Club (69-75-71-79=294), finished tied 1st with Al Spinoza – won 72-69=141 to 84-80=164 in 36-hole play-off
1930 at Interlachen Country Club (71-73-68-75=287), won by two strokes from MacDonald Smith

British Amateur

1926 at the Honourable Company of Edinburgh Golfers, Muirfield, lost in the sixth round to Andrew Jamieson Jnr 4 & 3

1930 at the Old Course, St Andrews won the final defeating Roger Wethered 7 & 6

British Open

1926 at Royal Lytham & St Anne's (72-73-74-74 = 293), won by two strokes from Al Watrous
1927 at the Old Course, St Andrews (68-72-73-72=285), won by six strokes from Aubrey Boomer and Fred Robson
1930 at Royal Liverpool Golf Club, Hoylake (70-72-74-75=291), won by two strokes from MacDonald Smith and Leo Diegel

These results can be presented in another way. In the lean years in the United States, the sum total is that he once reached the final of the US Amateur in five appearances and was once second in the US Open in three appearances. In the fat years, he won the US Amateur five times, losing in the final once, in eight appearances and he won the US Open four times, finishing second three times, in eight appearances. On the other side of the Atlantic, in the lean years he lost in the sixth round of the British Amateur and failed to complete his third round in the British Open. In the fat years, he won the British Amateur once in two appearances and won the British Open three times in three appearances.

The quality of opposition in both amateur and professional circles was very strong: in the amateur context it included Francis Ouimet, Chick Evans and George Von Elm and among the professionals were Walter Hagen, Tommy Armour, Gene Sarazen, MacDonald Smith and Leo Diegel.

In the 'fat' years neither Walter Hagen nor Gene Sarazen – players of the highest pedigree – won an Open in the United States or Great Britain when Jones was in the field.

Sports writer Charles Price described his record in yet another way:

> In the last nine years of his career, he played in twelve Open championships, nine in the United States and three in Great Britain. He finished first or second in eleven of those twelve starts. In six out of the last eight of those United States Opens, he either won outright or finished in a tie for first. In four out of the last – well, you could go on forever. Each time you hold Jones's career to the light, the more foolish it seems to compare anyone, pro or amateur, to him.

In his 36-hole singles matches in the Walker Cup matches, Jones beat Cyril Tolley by 12 & 11 at the Old Course, St Andrews in 1926; beat Philip Perkins by 13 & 12 at Chicago Golf Club in 1928; and beat Roger Wethered by 9 & 8 at the Old Course, St Andrews in 1930. As an example of the gulf between him and the others in the field, in the last three matches of the 1928 US Amateur he beat John B. Beck in the quarter-finals by 14 & 13, Phillips Finlay in the semi-final by 13 & 12 and Philip Perkins in the final by 10 & 9.

By 1923, the transformation from lean years to fat years was dramatic and complete. The *New York Times* indicated that the change of Jones from a 'petulant, irascible, passionate, explosive' youth to a 'model of sportsmanship, poise, and self-control' represented a 'splendid example of self-mastery.' There would appear to be several factors that brought about the metamorphosis. The one given the most prominence by Jones and by others is that he began playing against 'Old Man Par' (the par of the course) rather than against his direct opponent in match play or his several opponents in medal play. While winning the US Amateur in 1924 Jones said to Keeler, 'I have discovered that if you just keep shooting pars at them, they will all crack sooner or later.' Freed of the burden of striving for birdies, he became relentless in match play and more consistent in medal play.

Another technical factor that deserves more credit than it is generally given is the improvement in his putting. The 'Grand Old Man' of American golf, Walter Travis, watched Jones closely in his first appearance at the US Amateur in 1916. He concluded that the young man's putting method was faulty and invited him to come out half an hour before the morning match of the following day.

Unfortunately the party, under the supervision of Perry Adair's father, missed the earlier train and only reached the course as the matches were starting. Travis was known as a stickler for time and was not prepared to wait for the tardy youngster. Instead he had gone out on the course. The lesson he intended to give was instead given some eight years later.

In 1924 Travis watched Jones putting even less effectively than he usually did, while playing an exhibition match. Keeler was witness to the session in the locker room of Augusta Country Club that followed. Sidney L. Matthew has defined the contents of the lesson. Travis mapped out a number of changes he saw as essential. Jones was to have his feet so close together that the heels were almost touching. The putter was to be taken back with his left hand in a long sweeping stroke with what appeared to be hinged wrists working in opposition to each other – not an easy concept. He changed Jones's grip so the index finger of the left hand overlapped the right hand. Travis visualised the head of a tack protruding from the back of the ball and used the swing of the putter head to drive the tack into the ball; this was to be realised not with a sharp stroke but with a smooth and rhythmical motion, as though the putter swung back and floated through the ball.

Overall this collection of ideas and principles was a complex package. It was nevertheless taken on board. Within a season Jones's putting underwent such an improvement that from being one of the weaker putters among the top players, he became not only one of the most consistent but also the finest. Perhaps his most emphatic exemplification of the end result was the curling putt he holed at the last to get into a play-off with Al Spinoza at Winged Foot in the 1929 US Open. He was playing with Al Watrous, with whom he had played the last two rounds in the British Open at St Anne's three years earlier. In travelling twelve feet across the glassy surface, the ball broke ten inches but was so perfectly judged that Watrous commented, 'if the hole was but a four and a half inch circle on the green, Bob's ball would have stopped right in the middle.'

But this failed to explain the change from incandescent rage to coiled control.

Jones realised that he had reached a low point in 1917 at the exhibition match at Brae Burn, Massachusetts. He was aware that Alexa Stirling was the main focus of attention and knew he had 'behaved very badly when my game went apart.

I heaved numerous clubs, and once threw the ball away. I read the pity in Alexa's soft brown eyes and finally settled down, but not before I had made a complete fool of myself.'

The single event that was probably the greatest factor in initiating the transformation has attracted less recognition than it deserves. It took place in the 1920 US Amateur at the Engineers' Club on Long Island. In the semi-final, he lost heavily to Francis Ouimet by 6 & 5. A number of writers refer to the episode on the seventh green when a persistent bee repeatedly landed on Jones's ball, creating much hilarity. At one stage a marshal covered it with a megaphone whereupon it emerged from the mouth end and landed on the golf ball once more. The suggestion was that Jones came to realise that concentration needed to be unbroken. Keeler fancied, 'that insect flew away with a lot of Bobby's juvenile attitude towards what we call serious golf.'

The real significance of what was undoubtedly a major turning point in the process of transformation is more elusive. By this time the golf writer Al Laney, who had first met Jones in 1919, had developed a close friendship with the young Atlantan who was six years his junior. His exploration into the inner mind of Jones at that time is remarkably perceptive:

> When the Amateur Championship of 1920 approached,
> I had known Bobby for more than a year, becoming
> progressively closer to and more intimate with him. I was
> fascinated by his personality – so gentle, so intelligent
> and so pleasant in an amazingly mature way on a surface
> that concealed a strong, almost uncontrolled temper.

In young Bobby, passionate emotions were a chaotic mixture with first one and then another in control.

They were submerged most of the time, but at certain moments they threatened to dominate his personality, his view of himself and the outside world. It was generally believed that Jones during those years was merely going through a protracted period of adolescence. Those close to him knew how much more alarming it was. This gifted young man, perhaps because he was so gifted, had to wrestle with demons.

I sought almost daily contact with him at this time and especially tried to be close whenever possible on the golf course. Once I travelled with friends of his to a tournament in Chattanooga in on old Hudson automobile that got stuck on a long, rain-slick, red clay hill somewhere in North Georgia. I twice had the experience of seeing him to the very edge of malice in fierce outbursts that neither he or I understood.

I was afraid for him, for I had seen him flushed and shaking in a rage of sudden anger, then drained white a moment later in sudden fear at the nearness of evil. In a sense I shared his deep inner struggle to overcome what, with his intellect, he knew to be ignoble. He knew well that he was poisoning himself with anger, that he must find the inner strength to rise above it. To reconcile this side of his nature with the wonderful young person I knew him to be was a difficult thing for me.

As a consequence of his concern for Jones's well-being, Laney decided not to travel to Long Island but was startled by the transformation evident in Jones upon his return after losing to Ouimet:

> When Jones returned, I could see at once that he had changed and something was different. I tried to question him about this and about the Ouimet match. For a while he would say little more than 'Francis helped me. You know what I mean.' Early in our acquaintance I had questioned him at length about Ouimet, because I was eager to hear everything about Francis, and Bobby was the first person I had encountered who actually knew him. Most of what I got from him were statements like 'Francis is a fine man' and 'There's nobody like Francis.'
>
> After the return from Engineers, I began to have a certain, faint understanding. I began to see that the young Bobby had for Francis what amounted, if not to actual reverence, then to the greatest possible admiration for him as a human being. I was a long time getting it out of him, and I had to wait much longer to understand that this relationship with an older person of Ouimet's character was the most important thing in the young life of Bobby Jones. Nearly a lifetime was needed to know how this could be, but understanding began with his remark, 'Francis helped me' and with the feeling of vast relief with which it was said.
>
> I think now that it was at that very point, that very day when Jones, with his deep feeling for unspoken thoughts, first realized that his weakness could be his teacher, that

he could be strengthened and not enfeebled by the experience through which he was passing. There was an incident in that match with Ouimet at Engineers that infuriated Bob and caused him to lose control, and his admiration for Ouimet made him feel thoroughly ashamed of such an outburst in the presence of one he revered.

'But all Francis really said,' Jones told me later, was 'Let's just play golf, Bobby.' Francis helped him by being Francis in the same way as Bob many years later helped others merely by being Bob. I think there is little doubt that this exchange on the course was the beginning of success in Jones's struggle, the turning point in the 'critical match I thought I was losing', as Bob himself expressed it a long time later.

Once he had achieved actual maturity by overcoming this disturbing and dangerous element of his nature, Jones became the most 'balanced' person I ever encountered in sport, a rare harmonious unity of the inner self and outer self which had formerly been at war.

Jones also gave a considerable amount of weight to the ticking off he got from Jock Hutchison at St Andrews in 1921 when he left the green instead of waiting for his fellow competitors to hole out. He dwelt on this after returning to the United States and realised it really was time to take stock and make changes.

Evidence that Jones was succeeding in the transformation needed came at the 1921 US Open at Columbia. Seemingly out of contention after three rounds, Jones started strongly with three threes in the first four holes. Clearly on top of his game, he hit a long drive down the par-five 560-yard fifth hole, then suddenly hooked two consecutive shots out of bounds. Watching on in horror, Alexa Stirling saw the familiar red suffusion of face and neck, as his knuckles turned white from the tetanic grip on the club. Then he relaxed his hands, gave a smile of resignation, dropped another ball to score a nine on the hole. His 77 for the round left him in fifth place but he was comforted by the awareness that his evolving coping mechanism could work.

Keeler saw Columbia as proof that the tide had turned, noting that he firmly believed 'that this tournament at Columbia was the ultimate closing of one chapter in the development of this remarkable young golfer. Bobby finally gained control of his temper.'

One factor that helped Jones realise that he was now in control of himself came in 1922. In the semi-final of the US Amateur at Brookline he lost heavily to Jess Sweetser but was proud to discover how he could accept the outcome without blowing up. He wrote 'I just figured that I was playing the best golf I knew, and that Jess was shooting better golf, and that for the first time I was in absolute control of myself.'

But while Jones now appeared to others to be in control of himself and his game, this transformation came at a price. It increased the physical and mental strain of competing at the highest level. Chick Evans always felt that an element of anger enhanced performance, noting that 'the angry golfer gets a zip to his shots and the calm one loses the crispness so definitely needed for the sailing qualities of a well-judged shot.' While Evans felt that Jones was strong enough to stand the strain of anger, it extracted a far greater price than others realised.

Looking back on his playing days and the process of transformation he achieved, Jones commented that after 1918 he 'resolved then that this thing had to stop. It didn't happen overnight, but I managed it in the end, at least in tournaments.' He added, 'to the finish of my playing days I encountered golfing emotions which could not be endured with the club still in my hands.' He also recognised the importance of the first breakthrough, when he won the 1923 US Open at Inwood at the age of 21. He expressed his perception eloquently when he said, 'If the long lane had not turned at Inwood I think sometimes it would have gone straight to its end in the shadows.'

Looking back, Darwin summed up the matter well:

Bobby did hate missing a shot. Perhaps that's why he missed so few, for in the end that highly strung nervous temperament, if it had never been his master, became his invaluable servant. In his most youthful and tempestuous days, he had never been angry with his opponents and not often, I think, with Fate, but he had been furiously angry with himself. He set himself an impossibly high standard; he thought it an act of incredible folly if not a positive crime to make a stroke that was not exactly as it ought to have been made and as he knew he could make it.

In championships, reflected Darwin, he did subdue 'a naturally fiery temper till he played the game outwardly as a man of ice; but the flames still leaped up within.'

CHAPTER FIVE

On strain and destiny

Seventeenth-century Dutch artists who had established their reputations had an alternative to paying substantial bills or settling substantial loans – they could instead offer to provide a painting, often one that flattered the vanity of the recipient. Rembrandt used this strategy to pay off the loan made to him by Jan Six and the legacy left for the student of today is perhaps the finest portrait of that century. When his child fell ill, the artist Nicholas Pickenoy called in the celebrated Amsterdam physician, Dr Nicholaes Tulp. After the child recovered, Tulp accepted in 1633 the offer of the commission of a painting as an alternative to his fee. This was the era of the *vanitas* genre of paintings, when it was not just sufficient for a picture to be a good likeness. It also had to present an allegorical challenge, often touching on the purpose and frailty of life.

Tulp understood the need for symbols and emblems. In 1632 he had directed Rembrandt on the composition of the famous painting *The Anatomy of Dr Tulp*. Tulp also directed Pickenoy on the elements that were to make up this portrait. The subject was to be shown pointing towards a candle that was alight and burnt down to its midpoint, indicating how his own life was burnt away by an internal flame, as he dedicated his life to helping others. To emphasise this point, text on a tablet of stone included in the painting reads *Aliis inserviendo consumor* which might be translated as 'In serving others, I am myself consumed' or 'I am consumed by serving others.'

This concept would have struck a strong chord with Jones. He might well have taken the opportunity to rephrase the expression so that it would apply to himself. He would have said *Meo fato in paganica perficiendo, ipse consumor* – 'In fulfilling my destiny in golf, I am myself consumed.'

It is known that Jones often indicated his perception that there was a predestination in place as far as the outcome of golf tournaments was concerned. There is a distinction to be made between a sense of predestination and fatalism. The fatalist approaches an event with shoulders drooped, aware that the outcome is going to be adverse. One who recognises predestination as applying will enter the event with aspirations of success, but also have the ability to look back on it afterwards and recognise that on this occasion the result was the outcome of preordained happenings, such as a missed putt by himself or an outrageous fluke by his opponent. Predestination works both ways and creates an awareness that both success and failure can be set in place before the day dawns.

The first reference Jones makes to this aspect is in 1927 in *Down the Fairway*:

And very lately I have come to a sort of Presbyterian attitude towards tournament golf; I can't get away from the idea of predestination. I may have reasoned out the mechanical side; perhaps just a bit of the psychological side. But behind it all, and over it all, there is something I think nobody understands. It looks more and more as if this game is all in the book before a ball is hit; and you merely go through a championship as you were rehearsed to go through it, perhaps a million years before. Perhaps that sounds idiotic. Well, maybe you weren't rehearsed. Maybe you simply play a tournament like one of the Tony Sarg marionettes, with somebody over you pulling the strings.

In the case of the megaphone incident in the 1919 US Amateur at Oakmont, Jones accept that as predestined:

There was something about that megaphone blast that seemed to tell me, as clearly as I suppose the Angel Gabriel will call time on us one day, that this was not my turn. That's partly what I mean when I suggest a golf tournament is all in the book, before a shot is driven.

He could also sense when predestination was coming to his aid. In the semi-final of the British Amateur in 1930 he stood over a twelve-foot putt on the seventeenth green that he needed to hole to stay all square:

When I stood up to it I had a feeling I never had before. I felt all through this tournament something had been taking care of me and that however I struck that putt it was going down.

In the same event, in his earlier tussle with the mighty Cyril Tolley, three times his ball had been saved from going into trouble by hitting spectators. It seemed as though Jones was destined to win the Amateur.

There is also a case to be made out, perhaps for the first time in detail, for the contention that Jones also sensed that he had been given a destiny – a destiny that he was obliged to fulfil in the world of golf. Before he would be able to allow himself to be free from the ordeal of competitive golf, he sensed that he would have to complete some apparently unattainable goal. Only then would he be released to return to the simple pleasure of playing golf for fun.

The first indication he gave of sensing that he was, like the *Flying Dutchman*, condemned to pursue what might turn out to be an endless journey came in 1925. After winning the US Amateur for the second time, at Oakmont, Keeler noted what Jones said to him:

O.B., I suppose it is inevitable that anyone who engages in a championship competition in any sport should become aware of the record book and should have a desire to leave something of importance in it. Just now I have won either the Open or the Amateur in the last three years. I am now 23 years old and I can't keep fooling around with this thing much longer. I think if I could win one of these championships in each of the next three years, I'd be willing to call it quits.

Here is the indication whereby he recognised that only by fulfilling some kind of destiny could he obtain his liberation.

In later years it emerged that the first time the possibility occurred to Jones that the Grand Slam could be done was in 1926. In that year he had entered all four major events and won two of them. He sensed that winning all four was achievable, though he did not mention this feeling to anyone but Keeler.

Once he had made the key transformation, his game had moved onto a higher plane and certainly gave him the means of meeting the challenge. In Keeler's 'fat years' his record in the Open championships on either side of the Atlantic was exceptional. He entered the British Open three times and won three times. He entered the US Open eight times, winning four times and finishing second three times, with the only dip in standard occurring when he finished eleventh at Oakmont in 1927.

It should not be thought that winning the Amateur on either side of the Atlantic was an easier hurdle. At this time, the status of the British Amateur and the US Amateur gave the events major significance in the world of golf. Lowe notes that the final of the 1921 US Amateur between Chick Evans and Francis Ouimet was watched by 13,000 spectators, the final of the 1924 US Amateur between Bobby Jones and George Von Elm by 10,000 and the fourth-round match in the 1930 British Amateur between Jones and Cyril Tolley by 10,000, while some 20,000 watched the final of the British Amateur that year between Jones and Roger Wethered. Of the four major events open to a top amateur, Jones considered winning the British Amateur the most difficult challenge. His natural dislike of eighteen-hole matches inhibited his play. For an amateur, the thought of winning the Amateur and the Open on each side of the Atlantic in the one year was to all observers simply inconceivable. Jones sensed it could be done.

To do so he would have to become outstanding in both match play and stroke play. The extent to which he did this is revealed by looking at his record. After his metamorphosis from external outbursts to contained emotion (albeit at the price of internal destruction), Jones became close to unbeatable in match play. In 1924 he was the ripe old age of 22, and his subsequent match play record is simply remarkable. It warrants setting out in full.

In the 1924 Walker Cup at Garden City GC, New York he suffered his only Walker Cup defeat, though that was in a foursomes match when he and William C. Fownes lost by one hole to Michael Scott and Robert Scott, Jnr. In the second day singles he beat the redoubtable Charles O. Hezlet by 4 & 3. In the US Amateur at Merion the following week he won his five matches, each of which was over 36 holes. In the semi-final he was up against Francis Ouimet. His opponent certainly had the game to run him close, but Jones won by 11 & 10, before beating a fine player, George Von Elm, by 9 & 8 in the final.

In the 1925 US Amateur at Oakmont, only sixteen players qualified for the match play stages and Jones won his four matches, each match again being over 36 holes. He won his first two matches by the margins of 11 & 10 and 6 & 5. In the semi-final he saw off George Von Elm once more, this time by a margin of 7 & 6, before beating Watts Gunn in the final by 8 & 7.

In 1926 Jones made his second appearance in the British Amateur, on this occasion at Muirfield, and after progressing serenely to the last eight, lost to the Scottish Walker Cup player Andrew Jamieson 4 & 3. Although he concealed the fact at the time, he had considerable problems with acute pain in his neck that had required treatment before the match. In the 1926 Walker Cup at St Andrews, he partnered Watts Gunn in the foursomes to beat Cyril Tolley and his Muirfield conqueror Andrew Jamieson by 4 & 3, then beat Cyril Tolley in the 36-hole singles by 11 & 10. In that year, the first two rounds in the US Amateur at Baltusrol were over eighteen holes and subsequent rounds over 36. Jones won his first four rounds, beating Francis Ouimet once more in the semi-final, though this time only by 5 & 4. Although playing well, he lost in the final to George Von Elm by 2 & 1.

The US Amateur in 1927 at Minikahda Minneapolis was played under the same format as the previous year. Jones again won his first four rounds, beating Harrison R. Johnston by 10 & 9 in the quarter-final and the luckless Francis Ouimet by 11 & 10 once more in the semi-final. In the final he played Chick Evans, who some years earlier had won the US Open and US Amateur in the same year. Jones won by the crushing margin of 8 & 7.

The 1928 Walker Cup was played at Chicago GC Wheaten Illinois and in the foursomes Jones and Chick Evans beat Charles Hezlet and William Hope by 5 & 3. In the 36-hole singles he beat R. Phillip Perkins by 13 & 12. In the US Amateur at Brae Burn in Massachusetts, Jones won his first two rounds over eighteen holes, then in the subsequent rounds over 36 holes beat John R. Beck by 14 & 13, Phillips

Finlay in the semi-final by 13 & 12 and T. Philip Perkins, the 1928 British Amateur Champion, by 10 & 9.

In the 1929 US Amateur played at Pebble Beach, California there was a great shock throughout American golf when the young Johnny Goodman beat Jones in the first round over eighteen holes by one hole. Goodman later won the US Open in 1933 as an amateur, the last player ever to do so, and the US Amateur in 1937. Goodman was never embraced by the establishment and history has not given his play the credit it deserves.

In 1930 Jones crossed the Atlantic for the last time as a player and in the Walker Cup at Royal St George's partnered Dr Oscar Willing to beat Rex Hartley and Thomas Torrance by 8 & 7. In the singles Jones beat Roger Wethered, who had tied for the British Open in 1921 before losing in a play-off, and had won the British Amateur in 1923 by 8 & 7. In the British Amateur at St Andrews Jones had to win seven matches before reaching the final, where he once more beat Roger Wethered, this time by 7 & 6. The US Amateur returned to Merion, where Jones had first appeared in 1916 at the age of fourteen. He won his first four matches, beating former British Amateur Champion Jess Sweetser by 9 & 8 in the semi-final. He won the final, beating Eugene Homans 8 & 7, thereby completing what was at first labelled the Impregnable Quadrilateral and later the Grand Slam.

It is difficult to imagine what emotions were experienced by players who discovered that they were to play Jones the next day during this period. Johnny Goodman, then aged nineteen, made his way to Cypress Point for the 1929 US Amateur and was delighted to find himself drawn against his idol. He rose to the occasion, and losing in the next round was irrelevant to the young man. Of the others, some froze, some shrugged their shoulders and admitted the challenge was beyond them. Those made of sterner stuff came onto the first tee with resolve and proceeded to play to the best of their ability but still found themselves on the receiving end of a heavy defeat. The final of the 1925 US Amateur was for the only time in history between two players from the same club. Jones was impressed with the play of his young friend Watts Gunn and persuaded Watts's father to allow Jones to take the youngster with him to Oakmont. On the first tee of the final Watts Gunn asked Jones if he was going to give him the usual two shots per side, as he usually did in Atlanta. Jones looked him in the eye and retorted, 'I'm going to give you hell, you little s.o.b.' and did so, winning 8 & 7 earlier, despite Gunn playing to the best of his own game.

Looking back, one can only feel sorry for Francis Ouimet, who had the misfortune to run up against Jones in the semi-final of the US Amateur in 1924, 1926 and 1927. Ouimet had proved himself a steely competitor, having beaten Harry Vardon and Ted Ray in the famous play-off in the 1913 US Open at Brookline, and he was to win the US Amateur twice, his victories coming some seventeen years apart. Herbert Warren Wind recounted how 'once when I was talking to Francis Ouimet, an altogether modest and gracious man, about the long interval between his first victory in the Amateur, in 1914 and his second victory in 1931, he raised his voice to a dramatically emotional level, which was most unlike him, and said "Don't get me wrong, but I played some pretty darn creditable golf in the Amateur in the twenties, then I'd run into Bobby, and he would absolutely annihilate me. You have no idea how good Bobby was!"'

Ouimet revealed what it felt like to play against Jones when he wrote:

I can only describe a match against Bobby in this manner: it is just as though you got your hand caught in a buzz-saw. He coasts along serenely waiting for you to miss a shot, and the moment you do he has you on the hook and you never get off. If the young man were human, he would make a mistake once in a while, but he never makes any mistakes. He manages to do everything better than anybody else. He can drive straighter than any man living. He is perfectly machine-like in his iron play, and on the greens he is a demon. If you can beat that type of man, I should like the recipe. But he is more than a great golfer. He is a grand competitor.

British Walker Cup player Dr William Twedell won the British Amateur in 1927 and was to take part in a memorable final of the British Amateur at St Anne's in 1935 against Lawson Little. He gave an insight into the impact Jones inadvertently had on others. He wrote:

I really am unable to play my game, or what I call my game, when I know that Bobby Jones is playing on the same course. When he is on the course I feel I have no right to be out there going through the motions and playing golf. Since I watched him at St Andrews winning the British Open, I have had an inferiority complex.

I feel that there is no good reason why I should play golf. Bobby Jones is a supreme artist. The rest of us, and the best of us, are no more than children, stumbling around.

Talking about playing with Jones, Sarazen said, 'Bob was a fine man to be partnered with in a tournament. He made you feel that you were playing with a friend, and you were.' Having said that, playing with Jones was for many an unsettling experience. Chick Evans was a hardened player, having won the US Open and US Amateur in the one year, in 1916. He noted how intense Jones's concentration was: 'I noticed this in the final of the US Amateur at Minikahda three years ago. He only said two or three words all day long. He did not dislike me; he was merely out to win. It was a queer sensation. Bing! A sharp report and then he was away, lost in that gallery. Now and then I would see him in the center of that great mass, but his very expression said, "Do not speak to me! I have a job to do."'

With the clubs and balls of the time and the condition of the course, 72 was often a good score; a round under 70, while not unknown, was certainly not that common. One spell of play reveals just how good Jones had become and how wide was the gulf between him and the rest. It started at Old Elm Golf Club near Chicago, where he broke the course record the first time he played there. A few days later he played the Chicago Golf Club and broke the course record there. The following day he broke the record he had set less than twenty-four hours earlier. The next day he equalled the earlier record he had set on first acquaintance. A few days later, playing at Flossmoor, he started indifferently and was two over par after seven holes, before playing the remaining eleven holes in 3, 3, 3, 3, 3, 3, 3, 4, 3, 4, 4. His scores over twelve consecutive rounds were 69, 71, 69, 68, 68, 68, 67, 68, 67, 70, 69 and 67. And this was at the age of 26.

Now he had made the transformation in all aspects of his game, he had the opportunity to begin to meet his destiny, but could he survive the strain? By converting his internal equation from destructive outbursts to consuming erosion, he had given himself the means of achieving the ultimate level of play and success in the major events, but he sensed that the journey was going to take him to the edge of what he could endure.

From 1923 onwards, Jones was relentlessly victorious, but at a price to his physical and mental well-being. When he played in major events, he was repeatedly drained in a way that concerned close friends. Bearing in mind that his exposure to good weather had given him a face that was bronzed and exuded good health, for his appearance to be noticeably affected the changes must have been marked. Repeated observations by golf commentators indicate how pronounced the impact on his face was to others.

In the 1922 US Open, a concerned Keeler was trudging up the fourteenth fairway, weighed down by concerns about how Jones's round was wobbling. Someone clapped him on the back and said, 'Don't let your chin drag. It isn't as bad as all that!' When he realised it was Jones who was cheering him up, Keeler grinned and Jones 'grinned a bit too. But his face was gray and sunken and his eyes looked an inch deep in his head.'

At the same event, Grantland Rice commented, 'Even the people closest to Jones, those who had been with him for years and seen his blackest moods, were shocked by his appearance as he came off the course. The deep circles under his eyes and the weary sag of his body gave him the look of a man who had been mortally wounded.' Jones played the last hole of the 1923 Open at Inwood poorly for a six. Keeler went to offer encouragement as he walked off the green. 'His face gave me such a shock that for a moment I forgot what I meant to say,' he later recounted. 'His age seemed to double in that last half an hour.' Finally Keeler was able to say, 'I think you're champion.' The response from Jones was, 'Well, I didn't finish like a champion. I finished like a yellow dog.'

Before the next day's play-off against Bobby Cruickshank, Ouimet, who had roomed with Jones, told Keeler that the young man had slept well, but O.B. was appalled to see 'how drawn and pinched Jones's face looked, how his eyes seemed to be located in the back of his head.'

In the 1927 British Open at St Andrews, 'careful observers noted how drained Jones's face looked, how the shadows beneath his eyes seemed so dark, and more than one asked if he were physically unwell.' In the last round he wobbled over the first five holes before picking up four birdies starting at the sixth but 'his face was set and sunken and he never changed his expression.' The following year in the US Open at Olympia Fields it was noted that 'When it was over Jones's eyes looked no larger than pinpoints, and he was near to the brink of physical and emotional exhaustion.'

After Jones won the British Amateur at St Andrews in 1930, Fred Pignon wrote in *Golf Monthly* that 'He was pale and worn, and his usually immaculately brushed hair was tousled. The smile which seems to play forever about his features was gone, and the face looked lined and seared now after the weeks of strain and triumph had come.'

Grantland Rice watched him come in for lunch between the two rounds of the final of the 1930 US Amateur, the fourth leg of the Grand Slam, and asked himself, 'Has he ever looked as tired and spent as this? Seven holes up, the match in hand and he only wants one thing: for it to end.' And after it had ended, the appearance was 'tired, worry-worn, and looking older, so much older than his twenty-eight years.'

The strain that produced these outward signs had a comparable inward effect. In the 1919 US Amateur he lost eighteen pounds in weight and in future championships he invariably lost ten to fifteen pounds. As he himself pointed out, this was not the result of physical exertion. He could play 36 holes every day for two weeks with friends and not lose a pound, but in a championship 'the fire seems to be hotter.'

Writing in 1927, he commented on how Leo Diegel just missed out on winning in the 1920 Open: 'I watched Diegel play the last three holes, and I remember wondering why his face was so gray and sort of fallen in. I found out, for myself, later.' The year before, in the 1926 US Open, the effect of the physical strain came to a head on the morning of the final day. He woke up 'sick to the stomach' and asked a friend Bill Cairns if he knew a local doctor. They drove out to Upper Arlington where at 7am they woke up the household of Dr Earl Ryan. 'Doc, I've got Bobby Jones out here and he's sick,'

Cairns explained. Ryan gave him some medicine and Jones offered two tickets for the event. Ryan's response was, 'Just give me the ball you use today and we'll call it square.' The two men chatted for about forty-five minutes before Jones headed off to the course. After he won, he did indeed give the ball to Ryan and it became a family heirloom.

Knowing he needed a birdie four at the final hole of that 1926 US Open to edge past Joe Turnesa, Jones hit a huge drive of 310 yards that left him only needing a mashie at the 480-yard hole. Keeler describes how 'his knees were shaking so that he could hardly stand as he played that shot and they seemed to be buckling under him as he walked after it.' After getting his four, he dragged himself back to his hotel, not knowing if anyone might catch him and beyond caring. According to Keeler, 'Jones poured himself a drink, sat down, and burst into tears. "No more golf," his mother Clara Jones said sternly. For the first time in his life, Jones began to wonder if that was not such a bad idea.'

Recalling that moment, Jones admitted that 'I completely blew up for the first time in my life.' At the presentation ceremony he accepted the trophy without comment, having asked the officials not to call on him for a speech. The following year he wrote in *Down the Fairway*, 'And I can add earnestly that it is an aging game. Tournament golf, I mean. You may take it from me that there are two kinds of golf; there is golf – and tournament golf. And they are not at all the same.'

By 1930 the destructive impact of playing in championships was not only there for all to see but also causing concern to many. His Homeric struggle against Cyril Tolley in the

British Amateur, which was only resolved when Jones laid a stymie at the nineteenth hole, drained him profoundly. He wrote, 'It was the kind of match in which each player plays himself so completely out that at the end the only feeling to which he is sensitive is utter exhaustion.' He said at the time, 'I was neither exultant nor elated, just very, very tired. I suspect that Cyril felt the same way.' Having won the final against Roger Wethered and preparing to head to Hoylake, his comment to Keeler was, 'I'm awfully, awfully tired. I don't care what happens now.'

His play at Hoylake was a grim struggle. After he left the final green, George Greenwood tells how Jones 'flopped into a chair with his face as grey as stone and his cheeks fallen in. I never saw a man closer to the point of collapse than was Bobby Jones.' The exhausted player went up to the secretary's room to await the outcome. Keeler recalled how he 'went up to see him several times, and as often went down again to see what Mac Smith and Diegel were doing. On one of these visits I asked Bobby, bluntly, when he was going to quit this foolishness. That's the way it seemed just then – a tragic sort of foolishness.' Jones replied, 'Pretty soon, I think – and hope. There's no game worth these last three days. The tournament has taken more out of me than any other I ever played in.' Keeler went on, 'He told me later that when they called for him to go out on the lawn and get the cup, he hardly knew what it was all about. I think that right there he was deciding he had had enough, no matter what happened the rest of the year.'

Darwin was preparing his articles in the same room and described how 'I was writing in the room where he was waiting to know if he had won. He was utterly exhausted and had to hold his glass in two hands lest the good liquor be spilt. All he could say was that he would never, never do it again. He could doubtless have won more but at too high a price.' When he knew he had won, he was able to take one hand off the glass but the cost was there to be seen. Darwin concluded that 'Seeing him nearly past speech, I thought the time had come for him to call a halt and this game could not much longer be worth such an agonising candle. Golf had always taken such a prodigious toll and I now thought it had taken too great a one. The time to go, even at the age of twenty-eight, was fast approaching.' Later that evening Jones told the British press that he was so exhausted from stress and strain that he doubted he would compete in Britain ever again.

Moving on from Hoylake, the third stop in 1930 was Interlachen for the US Open. After one round Jones was so drenched in perspiration that Keeler had to cut off his tie so that he could get under a reviving shower. After he won, Jones was asked by Keeler the same question that had been posed at Hoylake. This time his answer was, 'I don't know but soon. I'm pretty sick of it.' Keeler later concluded that it was in the upper room at Interlachen that Jones decided that come what may at Merion, he was through with competitive golf.

Before Merion he was rushed into hospital with what was suspected to be appendicitis but was attributed to nerves. Usually he had no problem with sleep even during big events. His routine was two stiff drinks, the first while soaking in a hot bath – 'the most relaxing combination I know' – followed by a good dinner, a few cigarettes, some conversation with Keeler or others and lights out at nine o'clock. At Merion, sleep left him and he was pacing his room, smoking one cigarette after another, sick to the stomach 'as if jackrabbits were jumping up and down inside.'

After winning at Merion and completing the Grand Slam, he slumped in the locker room and said to Jimmy Johnston, 'What fun do I get out of tournaments? None. You are merely an exhibition. This is my last amateur tournament. After today I am through with competitive golf. The strain of golf is wrecking my health, stunting me in my business ambitions, and I am sick of it all.' That November he announced his retirement and Clara, his mother, said, 'I am glad his tournament golf is over. I am tired of seeing him go away from home in good health and come home worn and exhausted.' Jones said, 'I felt the wonderful feeling of release from tension and of relaxation that I had wanted so badly for so long a time.'

The above examination of the destructive effect of the strain Jones experienced during the eight successful years helps indicate the ordeal he confronted each time he played and sets the scene for his win at St Anne's. By 1926 the 24-year-old Jones had completed the metamorphosis from club-throwing stormy vulnerable youth to something frighteningly close to the perfect golfing machine. But he still had to put it all into effect on the international stage. St Anne's was to be the setting in which he did so.

Sadly, this chapter also reveals how little pleasure he was able to take in championship golf. From the complete picture between 1926 and 1930, it is possible to sense his inner state of mind as he searched for a way to fulfil his destiny. He knew that only by so doing could he free himself from the shackles of tournament play and go back to the other kind of golf he described in *Down the Fairway* – golf that was fun.

CHAPTER SIX

The second crossing

In 1926 there was an emerging contrast between the United States of America and Great Britain. The latter had emerged from the ravages of the Great War in a bedraggled state. The carnage inflicted on those who had made what was euphemistically described as the ultimate sacrifice meant that the outcome was a lost generation of young men. The financial impact of the war on the national exchequer was simply catastrophic. Just after the war, the epidemic of Spanish flu took the lives of more people than the war itself. The impact of these three aspects was that the country had been nearly brought to its knees.

On the other side of the Atlantic, the ravages of war were barely in evidence. The nation's finances sailed along serenely. For the middle and upper classes, exuberant hilarity was the theme of the day. Blissfully unaware of the Wall Street crash just three years away, those able to do so partied the night away.

The Walker Cup was to be played at St Andrews. Nowadays players traverse the globe without a second thought, but in the 1920s a trip from the United States to Great Britain was a major expedition. The six-day voyage by boat was just the beginning. Factor in the British Amateur Championship, the Walker Cup and the British Open Championship, with days of practice in between each event, and such a trip becomes a major expedition.

In Britain, the effect of grinding poverty stirred up the usually inert industrial classes to express their anguish. Historically this does happen in Britain every now and again, though surprisingly infrequently. The Conference of Trades Union Congress (TUC) met on 1 May 1926 and called a General Strike to start on 3 May in defence of miners' wages and hours. The mine owners wanted to reduce the wages of miners by thirteen per cent and increase their shifts from seven to eight hours. The miners felt this was unreasonable.

Meanwhile the amateur American players sailed for Great Britain on 5 May on the RMS *Aquitania*. The Walker Cup team was surprisingly young, with half the team under the age of 22. Roland Mackenzie was still in his teens. There was also however a seam of experience with Gardner, Ouimet, Sweetser, Watts Gunn, Guildford and of course Jones. While crossing the Atlantic, those travelling had increasing concerns about the worrying news coming in about happenings in Britain.

The next few days saw dramatic developments. The British government handled the situation in a heavy-handed way, muzzling the media and seizing all supplies of paper to hinder publication of the TUC's paper. They sent a warship to Newcastle and set out to recruit over quarter of a million 'special policemen'. Industry was quickly paralysed by men refusing to work in many settings. By 8 May police were making baton charges on rioting strikers in cities and the army was escorting food lorries through London. In Northumberland, strikers derailed the *Flying Scotsman* locomotive.

From onboard the *Aquitania*, William Fownes, the USGA President, sent a cable to the Royal and Ancient Golf Club of St Andrews asking for a report on the prospects of the events taking place and in reply received a rather tense telegram which stated: 'Shall try to carry out all the programme.' While on board ship, the Americans had kept their golf in trim, either by hitting balls into the ocean or by using a device with a ball attached by a string.

On 11 May 1926, the TUC, without consulting the miners, abruptly decided to accept the terms proposed by Sir Herbert Samuel, chairman of the Royal Commission on the Coal Industry, and called off the General Strike. Within a few days the whole event had petered out. Abandoned by other workers and left to their own devices, the miners struggled on alone for another six months, until they capitulated and went back to work for less pay and longer hours.

The American golfing expedition landed on 11 May, the same day the strike was called off, to find an absence not only of porters but also of the boat train. They had to rely instead on a charabanc arranged by the R&A to deliver them to the Savoy Hotel in London. When they reached London, they found tanks and armoured cars in the streets and helmeted troops on patrol. While there was evident apprehension in the atmosphere, British phlegm and stoicism meant life went on as best it could.

On terra firma, some found their land legs by playing in the Royal St George's Championship Grand Challenge Cup on 15 May. In appalling conditions, George Von Elm finished second behind Charles Hezlet. At nearby Rye the US Walker Cup team played a one-day exhibition, defeating the Oxford & Cambridge Golfing Society.

There may have been an agreement between the captains that press coverage ought to be minimal for what could be seen as practice matches. This might explain why the extraordinary events of 19 May, when the visiting Americans played against another society called The Moles, have remained practically unknown.

The Moles were a convivial gathering of British international golfers and at Woking they emphatically beat the American Walker Cup team by six-and-a-half matches to three-and-a-half over 36 holes of foursome. The Moles had treated them to dinner at the Savoy Hotel the night before and years of prohibition might have weakened the stamina of some of the American team, though others including Jones had found their own way of getting around the restrictions at home.

Those seeking to excuse the Americans for losing point out that the first time they saw the course at Woking was when they came down on the morning of the match. If it is assumed that the hangovers were evenly distributed between the teams, the results in the morning foursomes were emphatic, with a lunchtime lead of 5-0! R. Harris and Major Charles Hezlet beat Bobby Jones and Jess Sweetser by the considerable margin of 4 & 3, Torrance and Beck beat Francis Ouimet and J. Guilford by two holes, Layton and Gillies beat Robert

Gardner and Watts Gunn by 3 & 1, Powell and Murray beat George Von Elm and Roland Mackenzie by 4 & 3, and Fairlie and Roberts beat Standish and Waldo by 3 & 1.

The Americans rallied in the afternoon, winning the second series by three-and-a-half to one-and-a-half, but Jones partnering Watts Gunn could only manage a half against Beck and Powell. The home players were three holes down with five to play, but had a run of four consecutive wins, as can happen in foursomes, to stand one up on the last tee. Powell's second shot ran through the green, ending under a bush, and the visitors were relieved to come away with a halved match. This left Jones with no wins in two matches, a day's play totally out of character for him.

There was a small amount of press coverage. The *Milwaukee Sentinel* reported that the American team 'were overwhelmed in a series of foursomes matches against The Moles, an outfit of British Internationals.' Reporting in *Golf Illustrated*, Harold Hilton wondered if the run-up to the match was too much, noting that 'All this, with a dinner or two thrown in, is a severe ordeal for even well-trained golfers.' He observed that 'Mr. Jones was hitting the ball with all the old sweet rhythm, but possibly with a lower trajectory than when last here ... A wonderfully true pivot.' Unfazed by the result, the US players headed north to Muirfield, East Lothian for the Amateur Championship.

Safely arrived in Scotland, the American amateurs faced not only the Amateur Championship at Muirfield but also the Walker Cup at St Andrews. The initial schedule was that Watts Gunn, Roland Mackenzie, George Von Elm and Bobby Jones were to stay on to play in the British Open at St Anne's, while the rest of the Walker Cup team would return home. However, even before the Amateur, Jones was so homesick that he resolved to forego the Open and return with the main body of the US team. Back at home were his wife and daughter, who was just a year old. Soon after reaching Britain, he revised his schedule accordingly and made a booking on the *Aquitania* that was to sail two days after the completion of the Walker Cup.

Jones was comfortable with his game and at Muirfield he overcame his instinctive dislike of eighteen-hole matches. He moved steadily through his opponents and in the fifth round he came up against the defending Amateur champion, Robert Harris. For this encounter Jones was particularly keyed up. Keeler 'had seen him go out and play par golf like a machine and crush his opponents with a ruthless pressure, but I never saw him flame with the brilliancy he displayed against the luckless Scotsman. It was the first time an American and British champion had ever met in either country's championship, and Bobby went out and destroyed Harris most spectacularly.' He started with a birdie three, played the first nine holes in three under par 35 and won nine of the twelve holes that made up the match, winning emphatically by 8 & 6. He was now in the final eight and appeared to be unstoppable.

The next morning he was stopped in his tracks.

His conqueror was the young Scot, Andrew Jamieson. Some accounts appear to deprecate the merits of his victor, but Jamieson had also been selected to play in the Walker Cup shortly after in St Andrews. In his Walker Cup singles he was to beat the American captain, Robert A. Gardner by

5 & 4. By an intriguing coincidence it was Gardner who had put out the fourteen-year-old Bobby Jones in the 1916 US Amateur at Merion. In the foursomes, in partnership with Cyril Tolley, Jamieson was to go down to the Georgia duo Bobby Jones and Watts Gunn by creditable margin of 4 & 3.

Keeler describes him thus:

Andrew Jamieson, whom Bobby met the next day in the sixth round, was an inexperienced lad, not in good health, for which reason he had taken part in little formal competition. He was a boy of pleasing demeanour and somewhat eccentric golfing habits. He rode his bicycle back and forth to the Muirfield course and his brother caddied for him. He spent three hours the night before his match with Bobby putting on the practice green in front of his hotel.

And all this untried youngster shot at Bobby was a string of thirteen pars and one birdie, and Bobby, slack from his tremendous play of the day before, could not meet the blast. Jamieson never failed to get a chip close or a putt down, and took the great Bobby in the ratio of 4 and 3. Exhausted and with shattered nerves, Jamieson passed out of the picture in the afternoon with a round of approximately 85.

There was certainly nothing shoddy about Jamieson's play. He was under par when the match finished and only once in the round did he have anything that could be described as good fortune. This happened at the thirteenth, then a shorter hole than it is now. A pulled tee shot often stuck

on top of the hill, leaving a fiendishly difficult pitch, but on
occasion the ball might dribble and meander down onto
the green. Playing against Jones, Jamieson had built up a
lead that made his victory almost secure, until his tee shot
at this hole was hooked high onto the hill. Darwin tells how
'The crowd stood spellbound watching the ball as it hung
hesitating. Would it stay there? It hovered for a moment,
then, avoiding all impediments, urged on at every hop by
patriotic Scottish cheers, it began to topple downwards by
stages, almost coming to rest and then moving on again till
at last it ended its nefarious career on the green, and the
invading champion's last hope was gone.'

Writing at the time, Jones was careful to do nothing to
tarnish Jamieson's win. He summed up the match by saying,
'in fifteen holes he was never above par, and was twice below
it, granting that the first hole is a par 5, on the measurement.
I wasn't shooting par golf, but I wasn't so bad, at that. He just
beat me.' It was not until 1961 that Jones revealed for the
first time the untold story of the day.

In *Golf is My Game* some decades later, he tells how after his
fourth-round match against Harris, 'my confidence was quite
high and I feared no one left in the field except Jess Sweetser,
who was in the opposite bracket and could not be encountered
until the final round. This confidence was to get a rude shock
the following morning, for in the act of lifting my head off the
pillow, I pulled a grievous crick in my neck. I had been sleeping
on my left side, and as I lifted my head, I felt, and I am sure
heard, the muscle up the left side of my neck give a loud, rasping
creak like a rusty hinge. I realized in a flash that this was likely to
be the end of my participation in that tournament.'

How he dealt with this problem gives yet another insight into the generosity and consideration Jones repeatedly showed towards his opponents. He made Keeler promise that on no account would he say anything about the difficulty either on that day or in the future. Were the match to go ahead, Jones did not want Jamieson to sense he was playing against someone in adversity, 'nor would it be sporting to deprive him of the credit for a victory should he gain it.'

Before then there was a decision to be made – what Jones described as 'the most difficult decision I ever had to make with respect to a golf tournament – whether to play the match or default. Naturally, I did not relish the prospect of playing a tournament match in which I knew I should be severely handicapped. But I hated giving up after having come so far, especially when I had been playing well up to that point.'

With Keeler, he travelled to the course. In the absence of a practice ground at Muirfield, he had to wander down the eighteenth fairway and hit a few balls towards the tee. He found he was barely able to raise his hands as far as his neck: 'Just a few balls with a brassie told the story. I was being called to the tee, and there was no need for further delay anyway. I would go out and do the best I could, so long as I could lift the club at all.'

Even when revealing in 1961 the difficulty he had had in 1926, Jones still acknowledged how well Jamieson had played: 'Andrew Jamieson played exceptionally well – two under par for the number of holes the match lasted – and probably would have beaten me anyway. It was certainly no discredit and no accident to be beaten by a player of his ability. On the other hand, I was left with some reason for believing that things might have been different had I remained fit.'

He admitted, 'I felt pretty blue when Jamieson stopped me. And more than ever I wanted to go home. But here's the working of fate. If I'd been fortunate to go on through and win the British Amateur, I'd certainly have sailed for home a week later, on the *Aquitania*.'

Because of its bearing on the entire trip, it is appropriate to learn more of how he was thinking. He goes on:

Then I got to thinking that if I went home now it would look somewhat as if I was sulking over failure to win the British Amateur championship – the Lord knows I was disappointed, because I'd love to win it. But truly I wasn't sore. And I didn't want people to think so. Moreover, I remembered that I hadn't behaved very well on my first visit, five years earlier.

And I thought I'd like to stay over and show people I really could shoot some golf, at times. I hadn't showed any golf yet, except that twelve-hole burst against Robert Harris. And so I thought I'd stay on for the British Open, and try my best to show them a little golf. I had little enough hope of winning the British Open. No amateur had won it since 1897, when Harold Hilton's name went on the beautiful old trophy, five years before I was born. But I thought maybe I could make a decent showing, and anyway I was determined, no matter where I finished, that I'd not pick up this time ... The British are a wonderful sporting people, and I wanted them to think kindly of me and to believe I could shoot a little golf.

This extract not only gives a revealing insight into the mind of Jones but also shows the curious mixture of serendipity and destiny that together brought him to St Anne's for his date with history. He duly sent in his entry for the British Open and, with the American team, headed for St Andrews. The Walker Cup turned out to be, like the Battle of Waterloo, the nearest run thing. Of those who were later to compete in the Open, Watts Gunn beat the Hon. W.G. Brownlow by 9 & 8 in a 36-hole match, thereby gaining some revenge for his defeat at Brownlow's hands in the Amateur. The half gained by George Von Elm against the redoubtable Major Hezlet was critical in the outcome of the fixture. Jones emphatically found his game and saw off one of Britain's amateur stars, Cyril Tolley, by the embarrassing margin of 12 & 11, having been nine up after the first round.

At this stage Jones sensed how his game was falling into place and 'was rather glad I was to compete in the Open championship.' After a few days' practice at St Anne's he headed south to Sunningdale, Berkshire for the Southern Section qualifying rounds for the Open. There he was to stun all present in a happening that merits a chapter of its own, when he played the ultimate round of perfection. He afterwards said, 'Lord, I was happy after that round; and the one the next day, when I got a 68 to go with it, and led the field by seven strokes. You see, I felt I'd showed them a bit of golf. And that was why I'd stayed over.'

The arrival of the American professionals taking part in the Open at St Anne's was closer to the event. A few years earlier, Samuel Ryder, a wealthy seed merchant who played at the Verulam Golf Club in St Albans, had heard the rumour that the British professional Abe Mitchell planned to emigrate to the United States in 1923 to further his golf career. Mitchell had been the professional at Verulam, attempting to augment his somewhat meagre income. Ryder befriended Mitchell and the outcome was a remarkable three-year contract by which Mitchell became Ryder's personal golf tutor for £500 per year – then a substantial amount – with a further £250 per year for tournament expenses. Mitchell stayed in Great Britain and became established as one of the best home players.

Ryder was eager to create a match for professionals to correspond with the Walker Cup amateur match and seized the opportunity that presented itself in 1926 to bring his idea into effect. The R&A had introduced a pre-qualifying event for the Open to be played at Sunningdale. As a consequence a dozen American professionals planned to play there on their way from Southampton to Lytham St Anne's.

Earlier that year, Ryder invited Britain and America to put up a team for an unofficial match at nearby Wentworth and Walter Hagen accepted the challenge on behalf of the Americans. In announcing the event, the Press stated that Mr Ryder would present a trophy to the winning side. At this point a certain amount of chaos was introduced. The Americans had only docked three days before the match. Because of the delayed effects of the General Strike, the transport system was still disrupted. Three of the American team were unable to get to Wentworth and replacements were called in. The event became a somewhat 'relaxed and sociable affair' and the home team won by thirteen-and-a-half to one-and-a-half matches.

Ryder was pleased that his man, Mitchell, played well, beating 'Long Jim' Barnes by 8 & 7, and in partnership with George Duncan beating Hagen and Barnes by 9 & 7 in the foursomes. In the singles, Duncan easily beat Hagen by 6 & 5. Wild Bill Melhorn won the only point for the Americans and Emmett French had a half. As the late substitutes all had British passports, the result had to be seen as being of little significance and it was probably as well that the trophy mentioned had yet to be made and was therefore not presented. This match was the forerunner of the Ryder Cup, which was first played for in 1927.

Between the qualifying rounds and the Open, most American players enjoyed leisurely practice at St Anne's, but for Mitchell and Hagen something far more significant was at stake. One would be forgiven for assuming that the defeat inflicted on a number of the Americans in the international match might have diminished their prospects in the Open at St Anne's, but the intervening days following Ryder's match saw an upturn in American morale. The magazine *Golf Illustrated* advertised a challenge match over 72 holes between the 'two greatest match players in the world, Abe Mitchell and Walter Hagen.' After 36 holes at Wentworth, Mitchell was four up and must have fancied his chances of winning the £500 prize, at that time the highest amount ever offered for a match.

Hagen was not only a showman but also an astute observer of life and in 1920 at Deal had seen how Mitchell's composure crumbled after a long wait on the first tee. The second 36 holes was due to start at St George's Hill at 10.30 the next morning, but it was some thirty minutes later that Hagen sauntered onto the first tee. Once again Mitchell was rattled by a delay and within six holes the match was square. Although Mitchell rallied in the afternoon with a round of 67, he lost 2 & 1. There was clear animosity towards Hagen at the time, not only from the crowd but also from the Press. Henry Cotton noted that 'keeping Abe waiting won Hagen the match – and it went down badly with the crowd.' It is said that Ryder was so annoyed that he instructed the jewellers Mappin & Webb to model a statuette for the lid of his trophy on Mitchell, so that for all time Mitchell would stand atop the Ryder Cup. The antipathy towards Hagen was still evident at the St Anne's Open some weeks later.

CHAPTER SEVEN

The story of St Anne's

In 1874 the town of St Anne's-on-the-Sea simply did not exist. A businessman from East Lancashire, Elijah Hargreaves, stood on the sandhills like stout Cortez on a peak in Darien. His vision was for a new town to be the 'Opal of the West' where folk could 'take the waters'. The St Anne's-on-the-Sea Land Holding Company was quickly formed and early buildings were constructed.

In contrast, the town of Lytham had existed for the best part of a millennium and is mentioned in the Domesday book as Lethum. For several centuries it was a sleepy fishing village, at times ravaged by sweeping winter gales, but otherwise providing a meagre existence from the land or the sea for its few hardy inhabitants. The land was owned by the Clifton family, who lived at Lytham Hall and who had by the early 1800s acquired considerable wealth.

By that time two developments arose which were to change Lytham forever. The first was 'taking the waters', which had become a fashionable activity for the well-heeled in Victorian society. During the eighteenth century Lytham had acquired a reasonable name for this activity but its success was limited by its relative inaccessibility. The second development, which took place only 39 miles away, was the birth of railway travel. The opening of the world's first passenger railway took place on 15 September 1830. The accident-prone statesman William Huskisson, Member of Parliament for Liverpool, was still recovering from an operation for strangury. He ignored his physician's advice not to attend the opening and as he was greeting the Duke of Wellington, he contrived to have his leg mangled by the approaching 'Rocket' engine. He died from his injuries, thus becoming the first fatality in rail travel.

Over the decades that followed, the spread of the rail network triggered a major expansion in Lytham's prosperity. February 1846 saw the opening of the line from Preston, which terminated in Lytham. The line was only extended into Blackpool in 1863, running alongside the land that was to become the golf course of today.

Since the Industrial Revolution, many men had made considerable wealth in Lancashire. By the middle of the nineteenth century Liverpool was a massive port, exceeded only by London. Ships brought in cotton from the United States, having taken thousands of slaves from Africa in the opposite direction. The mines of Lancashire produced the coal that fired the cotton mills spread throughout the county. The mill owners sensibly looked to live well away from the industrial grime they had created and built their substantial residences in Lytham, facing out to sea.

Just twelve years after the birth of the town of St Anne's, the Lytham & St Anne's Golf Club was founded by nineteen members on 27 February 1886. The choice of name for the embryonic club was practical. The course was entirely within the limits of the new town, but no one would have heard of St Anne's! In contrast, Lytham was well known as an established holiday resort, so the composite name served a purpose.

The members used a room in the newly built St Anne's Hotel near the pristine railway station and a course was quickly laid out on the inland side of the railway line – so quickly in fact that it was decided to open the links on 6 March, just seven days after the club came into being.

The initiative for golf in the area came, unsurprisingly, from an exiled Scottish teacher, Alexander Doleman. He was a member of a well-known golfing family and had previously tried to generate interest for golf in nearby Blackpool. Failing to do so, he could often be seen playing solitary golf among the sandhills. In Lytham and in St Anne's he finally secured the interest of a number of local men. These were men of means and energy, who on seeing the potential for a successful venture embraced it and brought it into being. Among the early members were wealthy men from the Manchester area, including cotton mill owners and the owner of Boddingtons brewery. More locally, men such as Talbot Fair, John Mugliston, J. Marcus Rae and J. Stretton Fair reflected the Victorian ethos. These were men who were used to making things happen.

The fact that only Doleman and Talbot Fair had ever played golf before was no impediment. The first competition was played on 17 April and Doleman, seeing a need to give the others a chance, gave himself a handicap of plus 17, but still finished third. One can only admire Mr Fullagar who kept plugging away for his 244 gross, averaging over thirteen shots per hole.

Such was the dynamism of the membership that as early as 1887 a cup was presented for competition by members of recognised golf clubs and 30 players entered from Royal Liverpool, Formby, West Lancashire and Southport. Among the competitors was the great John Ball of Hoylake who scored a gross 77, his handicap of plus 7 giving him a net score of 84. He won the cup after an afternoon play-off and also the silver medal for the best gross. Within a year of its being founded the club had thus made its mark in the top amateur reaches in the region.

On 8 November 1890, the fledgling club made its first foray into professional golf, holding what is generally accepted to have been the first significant professional golf event in England. There had previously been a minor professional event held in 1885 within a competition for members at Hesketh near Southport. Only five professionals played – four were local and one was from Elie in Fife. In contrast the quality of the field at St Anne's was impressive. From St Andrews Old Tom Morris, Alex Herd, Andrew Kirkcaldy and Hugh Kirkaldy; from Bridge of Weir Willie Campbell; from Musselburgh Willie Park; from Carnoustie Archie Simpson; from Hoylake Jack Morris; and from Troon the winner Willie Fernie. Given the limitations in travel this was a remarkable attendance, which may have been a reflection of the aggregate purse of £53. It is likely that the enterprising membership paid for the players' travel costs. Special trains were laid on to bring in spectators from Manchester.

Earlier that year there had emerged the first indications that the club had no lasting tenure on the land over which they were playing and a search for an alternative began. On Sunday morning on 20 July 1890, the captain John Mugliston met Talbot Fair, Marcus Rae and T.H. Miller at Ansdell railway station near the present ninth green. They walked back to St Anne's and deemed the land to be favourable, though Doleman expressed initial reservations about its suitability. In 1891 the land over which the present course is based was acquired, though play was to continue over the original links until 1896.

The club's first professional was George Lowe, who was grandly described as Custodian of the Links. Formerly an assistant to Jack Morris at Hoylake, creating the layout of the new links was his first such undertaking. He did now however have the luxury of constructing it at his leisure, in contrast to the usual frenzy and haste at other clubs.

The members were eager to see the development of ladies' golf, and in 1893 made preliminary plans for an event open to ladies throughout the country. The Ladies Golf Union (LGU) was simultaneously in its formative stages with the indefatigable Issette Pearson of Lytham & St Anne's at the helm as secretary and the union was eager to create a national event. To avoid a clash, the Lytham & St Anne's Club forewent its own event and instead the first championship under the auspices of the LGU was held at St Anne's and won by Lady Margaret Scott.

Meanwhile work started on drainage of the land over which the new course was to be constructed and for the next three-and-a-half years, up to eight men worked daily.

In part the land was broken dunes, which readily lent itself to the formation of holes of character. On the inland side was land that had previously been farmed and this called for intervention by human hands to create holes of guile and cunning. The land over which was created the current first four holes and the latter parts of the fifteenth and seventeenth holes, plus the eighteenth, was the result of some five hundred years of sand deposition as the coastline and beach gradually shifted westwards. The gifts of nature were skilfully manipulated and augmented to produce a varied and challenging course for play with the gutta percha ball of the times.

The first competition over the new course was played during the winter of 1896, with the rooms in the St Anne's Hotel, now some distance away, still serving as the base for social activities. In 1897 the members rose to the challenge of building a new clubhouse.

At that stage golf was a minority game played by only a few and an appropriate clubhouse would have been a relatively humble construction. These captains of industry instead created the substantial clubhouse enjoyed by the members of today. It was, for its time, excessive and exuberant, but has since become a wonderful reminder of the calibre of the club's earliest Victorian renaissance men.

The new course was beginning to receive widespread acclaim. Bernard Darwin extolled the virtues of its putting surfaces and concluded with the observation that 'there is always a chance of too strong an approach being bunkered in a flower bed beyond the home green, to the great amusement of the spectators in the smoking-room window.'

The course George Lowe laid out was good enough to be host to one of the four rounds of the great professional foursomes match of 1905 between James Braid and Sandy Herd representing Scotland and Harry Vardon and J.H. Taylor representing England. This match was set up by two men. One was Edward Hulton, captain of the Lytham and St Anne's Club in that year and owner of the Hulton Press, which produced the *Evening Chronicle,* the *Sunday Chronicle* and the *Daily Dispatch.* The other was George Thompson, who owned Thompson papers. Each put up the then considerable sum of £200. Two stages had already taken place in Scotland at St Andrews and Troon before coming to St Anne's. The English pair started the day at St Anne's eleven shots up and 6,000 spectators, again brought in by special trains, followed play. After rounds of 74 and 75 against 74 and 71, their lead was down to seven shots as they moved on to Deal, where they were to finally win by a margin of eight shots. 1913 saw the return of the Ladies Amateur Championship, but it became evident that following the arrival of the longer-travelling Haskell ball, the course was no longer the challenge it needed to be.

Accordingly, in 1919 the club invited the celebrated golf course architect Harry Colt to undertake a major remodelling of the course. This was not, however, Colt's first contact with the course. George Lowe's course was opened in 1896 and in 1899 the Oxford & Cambridge Golfing Society (O&CGS) made their first Lancashire and Cheshire tour. Matches were played against St Anne's, Formby and Hoylake. While Colt is now remembered as the leading golf course architect of his time – creating or remodelling the likes of Sunningdale, Pine

Valley, Royal Portrush, County Sligo and Muirfield – he was a more than useful golfer. He reached the semi-final of the British Amateur Championship in 1906 and as a Cambridge man he took his place on that O&CGS 1899 tour.

The singles were played over eighteen holes and each match was played out to the end with a result of holes up or holes down. The O&CGS team contained some useful players. John Low was number one in their singles order, Colt was sent out as number two and number four was Bernard Darwin. They must have been startled to find themselves up against some heavy artillery. On the St Anne's team, the numbers one and two were John Ball and Harold Hilton, with twelve Amateur Championships and three Opens between them. Also playing were Norman Macbeth and John Mugliston. Mugliston, whose portrait hangs in the clubhouse Club Room, won his match by an impressive ten holes. Finding himself up against the irrepressible Hilton, Colt performed well to only lose by four holes. In the afternoon foursomes over eighteen holes, Colt and Low claimed a memorable result, beating Ball and Hilton by three holes.

Colt's first contact with the course at St Anne's seemed to inspire him in the matches later that week. Firstly, he beat the great John Ball by one hole in a 36-hole singles match at Hoylake, and secondly at Formby he won his eighteen-hole singles against W.B. Stoddart by ten holes and partnered Low once more to win his eighteen-hole foursomes against Stoddart and Crosfield by nine holes.

The changes Colt made to the course at St Anne's over a number of years between 1919 and 1925 were substantial. A new green was created for the third hole, some 50 yards beyond the original green. The old green at the fifth, set in a gentle crater, was replaced by the wicked raised green of today. The green at the sixth, also set in a more dramatic crater, was replaced by a new green further on. In place of the old short eighth and long ninth, the current challenging eighth and widely admired short ninth were created. The seventeenth green was moved, from just over the cross bunkers to its current location some eighty yards further on and to the left, creating the emphatic dogleg of today. The eighteenth was given a cunning pattern of diagonal cross-bunkering that makes it one of the great finishing holes in the world of golf.

Then as now, bunkering created most of the strategic challenge. In *Golf at its Best on the LMS*, Dell Leigh mentions 'the Machiavellian cunning of the artificial bunkers. I believe that very popular gentleman, Mr Pym Williamson (who recently celebrated, in tumultuous assembly, his twenty-first birthday as their Secretary) was responsible for most of these, under the guiding hand of the great H.S. Colt. But whoever it was they are as remarkable as they are numerous – remarkable in that nature did not put them there, but man; and yet they have all the appearance of the real thing – and all the terrors.'

By 1923 the Lytham members thought they had a course that was ready for the major events. That year, an event described as the Northern Championship and Daily Dispatch Cup was played there. Several American professionals, led by Walter Hagen, the defending champion, and including Johnny Farrell, Mac Smith and Gil Nichols, had crossed the Atlantic in the *Aquitania* to play in the British Open at Troon and had decided to play the St Anne's event as well. Also with the American party was Gene Sarazen, US Open champion in 1922 (when he finished ahead of runner-up Bobby Jones). From Sarazen's account, there is an indication that what kept him in London while the others travelled north was the Italian hospitality he enjoyed at the Piccadilly:

In London I stopped at the Piccadilly Hotel. The manager was an Italian, and when he discovered that we had a common ancestry he insisted on putting me up in what amounted to the bridal suite and assigning the aces on his staff to see that everything was 'top-hole'. I was happy to assure him from time to time that everything was ripping. Along with the other American visitors, I played some charity exhibitions in and around London for a hospital drive with which the Prince of Wales was connected, and then I went up to Scotland to fill some exhibition dates in the area around Perth and Carnoustie.

I returned to my acreage in the Piccadilly and there discovered that the other boys had already gone to Lytham and St Anne's, a course outside of Liverpool, to play in the North of Britain championship. I wired them that I was going to pass up on that tournament in order to devote all of my time to getting ready for the Open.

The crowd at St Anne's, Hagen in particular, kept telephoning me at all hours. If I was imbued with the true competitive spirit, Hagen told me, I would not be afraid of what would happen to me in a field composed of such illustrious players as Harry Vardon, Ted Ray,

George Duncan, Abe Mitchell, J.H. Tayor, Jim Braid, Sandy Herd and Walter Hagen. I took the night train to Liverpool on the eve of the tournament. I won it.

While Sarazen, writing some years later, indicates that he was in London when he was summoned by his fellow Americans, an article in the *Scotsman* on 2 June 1923, suggests a different angle. The report reads:

> It was only at the earnest request of his fellow-Americans that Gene Sarazen competed in the North of England Championship. With typical American thoroughness he was practising at Troon, but he was prevailed upon to journey south to St Anne's by his countrymen.

Hagen must have regretted dragging Sarazen to St Anne's as the final score showed Sarazen finishing first and Hagen second, two shots behind. The members must have been pleased to have the current US Open champion in first place and the current British Open champion as runner-up.

For Sarazen, a greater delight than winning was playing the first 36 holes with 'the peerless Harry Vardon'. The young American admired the play of Vardon, now aged in his early 50s, from tee to green, but was saddened by the experiences of the older man on the greens. Sarazen wrote:

> In one of the rounds Vardon had a 73 and I have never seen a man putt worse. He was stabbing everything. On one green he had a 3-foot putt and hit three inches behind the ball. He walked off the green without a

word, as if he felt a little embarrassed for such an exhibition.

Vardon liked my style of play, he told me. 'If I were you, young man,' he said after I had punched a one-iron into a cross-wind and on to the green at a difficult short hole, 'I would never allow for the wind. You hit the ball very sharply and have a natural low trajectory to your shots. You should always play right for the pin.'

The course had thrown up a worthy winner but the scoring was perhaps on the low side. A few weeks earlier in the Daily Mail Tournament, James Ockenden and Len Holland had scored 68s and in the North of England Championship Sarazen returned a 68, but H.A. Gaudin of Jersey had a 67, thus earning £100 for the first professional to beat the recent record, £25 for the best round of the meeting and £25 for the best round by an ex-Service man. In those days, winning £150 in a single round was a good return, especially for one who was not the overall winner but finished tied for third. His four-round total of 293 was equalled by the home club professional Tom Walton who had rounds of 73, 75, 73 and 72.

Further down, Ted Ray finished in eighth place on 298 with Joe Kirkwood on 300, and Jim Barnes and Johnny Farrell both on 302. Despite his putting woes, Harry Vardon had a commendable 303.

The R&A were invited to consider the course as an Open Championship venue, but shocked the club by responding that the course was not sufficiently difficult. Harry Colt made further adjustments and the corresponding event in 1925 was won by Abe Mitchell, with a 72-hole score some fifteen shots higher than Sarazen's. A further approach was made to the R&A, meeting this time with a positive and favourable response, allocating the 1926 Open to the club.

All was set fair for the Lancashire club to host the oldest golf championship in the world.

CHAPTER EIGHT

A glimpse into the hall of Valhalla

Valhalla: 1. Norse mythology – in the after-world of Asgard, which was ruled over by Odin, there was a majestic hall called Valhalla. Of those who die in heroic combat, the bravest were selected by the Valkyries and led to Valhalla, where they awaited the Last Day. There they were sustained by mead which flowed in the place of milk from the mighty goat Heidrun. Each evening, the cook killed the great boar Saehrimnir and the warriors feasted on his flesh, but he was restored to life the following morning. The heroes were to dwell in Valhalla until the future great and final battle of Ragnarök, when they would march out of the 540 doors to fight at the side of Odin against the giants.

2. A place of honour, glory and happiness.

FROM *THE SAGA OF ASGARD*

In the aftermath of his defeat at the British Amateur at the hands of Andrew Jamieson, Jones's mind was at first in a spin. His initial plan had been to play in the Amateur and the

Walker Cup, then to stay on with his friend Watts Gunn to play in the Open. But as Keeler notes, 'Even before the British Amateur, Bobby got homesick to a degree that caused him to abandon the idea of staying over for the British Open. He had left behind him his wife and a little daughter, a year old, and the rest of his family; and soon after reaching Britain he had booked a return passage on the *Aquitania* with the other members of the Walker Cup team who were sailing two days after that match.' Losing in the sixth round of the Amateur called for a rethink.

He was now aged 24 and had won the US Open. But was he good enough to win on the larger stage? He remembered his previous trip to Great Britain in 1921, with abject defeat in the Amateur at Hoylake and ignominy in the Open at St Andrews, when he picked up his ball at the eleventh hole in the third round. Links golf had baffled him on that expedition. Now he was wiser and more experienced, yet his performance on these mystifying courses did not live up to the demanding expectation he made of himself.

Perhaps his game wasn't yet ready for this sphere of play? Perhaps he should enjoy being back with his family now? But the fire which ceaselessly drove him on overwhelmed such thoughts. He had to follow his destiny and the luxury of being back home would have to wait. At the same time he knew his game was off-key and there was no way of knowing if the much-needed element of improvement would happen.

Just after his defeat in the Amateur at Muirfield, Jones was described by Keeler as 'pretty blue and more than ever he wanted to go home.' It was therefore to some extent with a heavy heart that he decided on 5 June, before the Walker

Cup, to extend his stay and submitted his entry for the Open to be played over a course unknown to him at Royal Lytham & St Anne's. Jones told Keeler that if he didn't compete in the Open, 'It wouldn't be sporting. It would look as if I was sulking because I didn't win the Amateur.'

Shortly after making that momentous decision, there was evidence that Jones's game, until then decidedly scratchy, had undergone a degree of transformation. In the Walker Cup he partnered Watts Gunn in the foursomes to a 4 & 3 win over the splendid Cyril Tolley and his earlier conqueror Andrew Jamieson. In his singles he beat Tolley by the massive margin of 12 & 11 in a match scheduled for 36 holes. He then travelled to St Anne's to familiarise himself with the course, but his play in practice there was distinctly moderate.

From there it was off to Sunningdale, Berkshire, to qualify from the Southern section of regional qualifying. There, two developments occurred. Jones felt an immediate affection for the course and had two rounds of 66 in practice. Perhaps more importantly he picked up a 'beautifully modeled' driver from the Sunningdale professional, Jack White, who had named the club Jeannie Deans, after a Scottish heroine from Walter Scott's novel *The Heart of Midlothian*. The driver seemed to inspire Jones and he never played with any other driver in competition thereafter, winning ten Majors with it.

In the first qualifying round at Sunningdale, Jones played what was quite simply the nearest thing to a perfect round ever played by anyone before or since. Those who witnessed it were stunned. The next day the incomparable Bernard

Darwin, writing in *The Times*, gave an insight into just what had happened:

By now it was 4 o'clock, and nothing else mattered except the watching of Mr. Bobby Jones, who was drawn with a venerable and illustrious namesake, Rowland Jones.

Mr. Jones had certainly done one 66, and rumour says two, round Sunningdale in practice. Nevertheless he was not quite satisfied with his game and was assiduously practising with different drivers before the round. Clearly he had found out the secret, for he at once began to play such golf as has never been seen on the course. It was perfect, and that is all there is to be said about it; so perfect, indeed, that at times its sweetness was almost cloying. However, there is an antidote. Go and stand as close as you can to Mr. Jones; see and almost feel the swish with which the club comes on to the ball and the great thrust of the hips which accompanies it, and you realise what force is concealed by that apparent caressing gentleman. Mr. Jones missed a 4ft. putt for a 3 at the third and a 5ft. putt for a 3 at the ninth. On the other hand, he holed quite a long putt of six or eight yards for a 3 at the fifth. Otherwise it would be a waste of words to describe his first nine holes.

At the tenth he played one of the very finest shots I ever saw in my life, a huge hit with a No. 1 iron, as straight as an arrow over all the bunkers, to within six yards of the pin. He ran up to 5ft. and got a 3 at the 11th, and was within inches of another at the 12th. The short 13th was memorable because he actually made a bad shot, pushing his ball out into a bunker, but he recovered beautifully and down went another five-foot putt for another 3. Even for so habitually faultless a player the strain must have been getting great, and Mr. Jones began, I thought, to look rather hot and tired, but the golf went on exactly the same plane. He was putting for a 3 at the 14th and a 2 at the 15th. At the 17th he actually pushed his drive a little off the fairway, but he was putting for the same old 3 nevertheless. He got his 4 with consummate ease at the last hole, and so, amid reverential cheers, finished in 66, a score consisting entirely of 4's and 3's.

After that the crowd dispersed, awe-stricken. They had watched the best round they ever had seen or would see, and what the later players did they neither knew nor cared.

To match the occasion, this was golf writing of the highest order.

Charles Macfarlane, writing in the *Evening News*, noted that the 66 was made up of 33 shots out and 33 shots in, with 33 putts. He commented:

This proves how truly wonderful his golf was. His exhibition was, indeed, the finest I have ever witnessed in my long acquaintance with the game. Even Harry Vardon, when he swept the country of records and medals and won championships, did not play better golf than this little American wonder golfer. His score made a record for the course. At all times it is a difficult course, but Bobby Jones made it look so simple – too simple, in fact – that many men spectators were driven to say that they would give up the game.

His second shot to the seventeenth was played from a rough lie, slightly off course. Had the club touched the heathery rough the shot would have been a poor one. The lie demanded an absolutely clean shot. Bobby Jones, when I asked him, thought that his best shot was that to the short fifteenth (short, that is, for some golfers); for, with only a vestige of wind to aid him, he drove the ball with his driving mashie nearly 230 yards.

His driving from the tee was a surprise to everyone. Seldom have I witnessed cleaner or straighter or longer hitting. The boy's game was perfect and chaste as Grecian statuary.

Macfarlane would later be given the club with which Jones played the famous shot at the 71st hole of the Open at St Anne's.

The second qualifying round could have been an anti-climax but the standard of Jones's play was not far behind that of the first round. Within his report Darwin notes:

There was chalked up on the score board the announcement 'Mr. R.T. Jones 134' and I should be glad if this article could consist of exactly those words. It seems so futile to say any more. Ten under 4's for 36 holes, 66 and 68 for two rounds of Sunningdale at fullest stretch, one 5 and one 2 and the rest of the 36 holes 4's and 3's. Say it how you please, you can add nothing to the incredible and indecent fact.

Mr. Jones compelled attention by doing a 68 and once again the wonder was, not that he did it, but that he did not do better, for his putts were all round the hole without dropping in. No figures and no description can properly convey the nature of his golf. There were many experienced golfers watching him and I think they agreed that such a player of golfing shots they had never seen in their lives.

George Greenwood writing in the *Daily Telegraph* threw more light:

Having made his position safe with a first round of 66, Mr. Jones was not bothering his head very much about the second. Still the 4's and 3's poured unceasingly from his magical clubs, like eggs from a conjurer's hands.

It really seemed as if Mr. Jones could not help himself. He just planted his feet on the ground, rather close together, put the clubhead down, swung it quite leisurely and away went the ball as straight as an arrow. It was not only golf of a stupendous order; rather was it enchanting, sweet and inexpressibly delicious. Never in the long history of the game have two such perfect consecutive rounds been played, and I doubt whether the like will ever be seen again.

'Thank you, thank you ever so much,' said Mr. Jones, smiling radiantly, as I congratulated him on the completion of his second 'wonder' round. 'I am more than glad; I am, indeed, happy that I have played well,' he added. 'I only hope,' he said, laughingly, 'that I have not shot my bolt before the championship actually begins.'

From the description Jones gives in *Down the Fairway*, it is clear that the round at Sunningdale had a profound effect on him. Writing in 1927, with three years of competitive golf still to come, he describes the round as 'the best round I ever played in important competition.' In the following years, he never equalled or surpassed it. He shows both affection and regard for the course, saying, 'I liked it so much I wished I could carry it around with me; it suited my game so delightfully.'

Nowhere else in all his writings does Jones take the reader through a round from first tee to eighteenth green. He did so in *Down the Fairway*, perhaps sensing that in his round at Sunningdale he came as near to playing the perfect round that either he or any subsequent player would ever come.

It is worth noting that he only holed one putt of any length – of 25 feet at the fifth – against which he missed from five feet at the third, from ten feet at the seventh, from five feet at the ninth, from seven feet at the eleventh and from twelve feet at the fifteenth.

His description is as follows:

The holes are given with their length, the American par, the clubs I used, and the score of my best round in competition.

No. 1, 492 yards, par 5. A drive and a brassie. Two putts. Score, 4.

No. 2, 454 yards, par 5. A drive and No. 1 iron. Two putts. Score, 4.

No. 3, 292 yards, par 4. What is called a mongrel length. Drive and wee pitch to five feet from the pin. Missed the putt for a 3. Score, 4. This was not the type of pitch I dread.

No. 4, 152 yards, par 3. A mashie, 25 feet from the pin. Two putts. Score, 3.

No. 5, 417 yards, par 4. Drive and No. 4 iron to 25 feet from the pin. One putt (the only long one of the round). Score, 3.

No. 6, 418 yards, par 4. Drive and No. 4 iron to 18 feet from the pin. Two putts. Score, 4.

No. 7, 434 yards, par 4. Drive and No. 4 iron over hill to 10 feet from the pin. Missed putt. Score, 4.

No. 8, 165 yards, par 3. The others were using a mashie here. I used the no. 4 iron and an easy swing, shooting for the centre of a dangerously guarded green, 40 feet from the pin. Two putts. Score, 3.

No. 9, 270 yards, par 4. Another mongrel, very interesting. A drive that rolled over the back of the green. A chip to five feet from the pin. Missed the putt. Score, 4.

This put me out in 33 with 17 putts and 16 other shots and not a pitch except the wee one at no. 3. It was three strokes under par, based on the yardage.

No. 10, 469 yards, par 5. A drive from a hillside tee to a valley and a stiff iron shot to an upland green. My shot with a No. 2 iron was 30 feet from the pin and I was down in two putts. Score, 4. [N.B. Darwin described the shot to the green as having been played with a No. 1 iron]

No. 11, 296 yards, par 4. Apparently too short for a good hole, but very interesting; a blind hole with much grief if off line. I chipped to seven feet from the pin and got the putt down for a birdie 3.

No. 12, 443 yards, par 4. A drive and iron to 30 feet from the pin and two putts. Score, 4.

No. 13, 175 yards, par 3. A no. 4 iron and my first mistake of the round; I think the only one. I shoved the shot out a bit to the bunker at the right, chipped six feet from the pin and holed the putt.

No. 14, 503 yards, par 5. A drive and brassie to the left edge of the green, pin-high. Two putts. Score, 4.

No. 15, 229 yards, par 3. A driving-mashie 12 feet past the pin, well on line. Missed the putt. Score, 3.

No. 16, 426 yards, par 4. A drive and iron to 40 feet from the pin. Two putts. Score, 4.

No. 17, 422 yards, par 4. A slight dog-leg to the right. A drive into the angle and the short rough and a No. 4 iron 30 feet from the pin. Two putts. Score, 4.

No. 18, 415 yards par 4. A drive and mashie 30 feet from the pin. Two putts. Score, 4.

This gave me a score of 33-33=66 against a par of 36-36=72, with 33 putts and 33 other shots, only three of them being pitches of any description, and not one of them a pitch of the type that has come to be something like a bête noire to me. The Sunningdale course is 6472 yards on the card as we played it that day, and the setting of the tee-markers made it a good deal longer at some of the holes than the figures given, which are taken from the card.

Jones's concern that his game had peaked too early was mirrored by Keeler. After the first round he noted that evening how Jones was 'a bit nervous and, as the saying is, keyed up. And he and George Von Elm and Archie Compston and I set out for a walk in the cool, long English twilight, and we wound up walking around the lake. We didn't know when we started that it was ten miles. We got in just at midnight. Bobby slept pretty well, after that stroll.'

While happy to have achieved golfing perfection, Jones was 'happy and worried. I had sense enough to know I had come to the top of my best game six days before the championship, which is where I would need it … Golf's a queer game. It comes and goes, and you cannot hold it. Anyway, I can't.'

Keeler went on to say:

I was worried, and so was Bobby. The Sunningdale performance meant he had come onto his game a week too soon. The place for such rounds was in the Championship proper – only one never seems to get them there.

He was gratified by the improvement in his iron play, as shown at Sunningdale, which necessitated a lot of it; as I recall, Bobby used a mashie twice and a mashie-niblick once for approach shots in the 36 holes; as suggested, Sunningdale was a long course. Most of his shots to the greens were good bangs with the irons, sometimes a spoon, and occasionally a brassie. Sunningdale was no drive-and-pitch affair, such as phenomenally low scores are usually are made on.

But we both realised that Bobby had come too good too soon.

It was time to head off to St Anne's.

CHAPTER NINE

Final preparations

Following the rejection of the course as an Open venue by the R&A in 1923, course architect Harry Colt was invited to make yet further changes. Mostly these consisted in tightening up the pattern of bunkers around the greens. In September 1923, he suggested that a new sixth green be created some forty yards beyond the existing one, which was a punchbowl green in a hollow just beyond the cross bunkers. The outline of the 1896 green can still be made out today.

The *Glasgow Herald* commented that in 1925, when the British Northern Open was again played at St Anne's, the course, compared with 1923, 'had been lengthened, a new and elaborate scheme of bunkering carried out, and the greens so guarded that nothing other than a perfectly played pitch was of the least avail. Moreover, the greens under a prolonged spell of sunshine were as slippery as glass, and the harder conditions were reflected in Mitchell's winning aggregate of 305.' As mentioned previously, this was fifteen shots more than Sarazen had needed two years earlier.

In the same article there was mention of a previously unknown aspect of the way the course was prepared for the 1926 Open. Since 1925, 'low ranges of sandhills have been constructed, and so cunningly constructed, too, that you can hardly tell the artificial ones from those put there by Nature. But the biggest improvement is the construction of wastes of sand by tearing up the turf in what were once long areas of thick long grass, and opening up the sandy subsoil to the sky. It has made better hazards and given the seaside character to the course which it ought to have, bordering the sea as it does'.

It was from an area prepared by this means that Jones would on the 71st hole play one of the greatest shots ever played under the amount of pressure involved at that stage of any event. The *New York Times* correspondent Spalding gave his readers a flavour of the course awaiting the players:

> The course, to use Bobby's words, is very tight. The fairways are narrow and are flanked in those places where the ball is likely to come to rest with vast tracts of sand, and the bunkers are omnipresent.

Yardage was then a less precise matter than now; tees seemed to be moveable feasts. 'The course is stretched out to its fullest extent and probably measures 6,600 yards,' wrote Spalding. 'There are four one-shot holes, ranging from 223 to 161 yards. All are very fierce, especially the fifth, which will be played beam on if the wind holds. Much sapping and mining will be carried out before the ball rests on this green.' The yardage of the eleventh is variously given as 601 or 599 yards, though

Spalding has it at 620 yards. He wrote, 'The latter is the longest hole on any championship course. In order for a player to get the easiest line for his second shot, he must carry a chain of sandhills of capital S formation at a point 200 yards distant. The prevailing wind is against the players, who need three hits off the meaty part of the club every time to get there.'

The American reader was told that 'the course at one time was noted for its long grass and lost balls and lost tempers.' Confirming the *Glasgow Herald*'s report, the *New York Times* described how 'the long grass has been got rid of by wholly removing the subsoil and exposing the sand beneath. Vast Saharas are everywhere. The course cost a pile of dollars, but there is enough and to spare among the members, who are textile magnets [*sic*] of Lancashire and Yorkshire and who live in big houses overlooking the course. It is enclosed and private and the Championship Committee is charging gate money.'

In the British Open the previous year at Prestwick, vast uncontrolled crowds swamped the course in their eagerness to see the popular American player Mac Smith win. Five shots clear after three rounds, victory seemed assured. In the meantime, Jim Barnes posted his last round of 74 for a four-round total of 300. An unmanageable crowd made play for Smith an ordeal and he staggered home with a last round of 82 to finish in third place. Prestwick never saw the Open again. Charging spectators for admission to the course was introduced for the first time at St Anne's in 1926 to deal with this problem.

While Jones was qualifying at Sunningdale in the Southern section, others played in qualifying rounds held for the

Central section at St Anne's. Hagen led with 143, one ahead of Tom Williamson of Nottinghamshire and three ahead of Jose Jurado of Argentina. There were two 71s and three 72s returned by the field. Concerns about the course being too easy were assuaged. American amateurs Roland Mackenzie and Jones's friend Watts Gunn both qualified at St Anne's, while George Von Elm qualified at Sunningdale.

After returning from his surreal trip to Sunningdale, Jones settled into a steady pattern of practice, with four consistent rounds of 72, 72, 70 and 71. It was noted he was 'still bunting the ball down the middle of the fairway, and, moreover, looks as if he could go on reeling off fours till the end of time.'

Bernard Darwin's first experience of St Anne's had been when playing for the Oxford & Cambridge Golfing Society on its first Northern tour and he developed an enduring affection and respect for the course's virtues. His *Country Life* preview of the 1926 Open pointed out that 'about the charms of the course there may be different opinions, but there will, I imagine, be none on one point, namely, that it provides an extremely severe and up-to-date examination in the art of golf. Everything has been tightened up; the holes are very long and surrounded, picturesquely speaking, by minefields of bunkers.'

A leading home player feared that his additional power would not repay him at St Anne's. He felt that 'the bunkers near the green were, in his judgment, so close and severe that the fact that he could reach the green in two shots, while other folk could not, would prove a hindrance rather than a help.'

The course changes generated mixed feelings for Darwin: 'One can never overcome some feelings of regret at changes made in courses that are old friends. St Anne's is an old friend of mine, and a very kind one.' After describing his good fortunes when playing in times past, he notes:

> I have, therefore, a tender feeling for the course and I was especially fond of the old crater greens in which it was rich. They were productive of such exciting moments of expectation, such heavenly flukes. But, of course, they had to go. The fifth I remember as a rather mild, easy short hole in a dell. It is anything but mild now, for the flag is perched on a narrow, guarded and defiant plateau, waiting to be won. The second and third holes were quite pleasant and required reasonable accuracy, but yet were comparatively anaemic. They are full-blooded holes to-day, for there is a terrifying carry from the second tee, and the third green has been carried into some admirable hilly country. I could go on, but fear to grow tedious. Enough, then, that St Anne's is a fine, long, difficult course, and the man is not born who can play four rounds of it without getting into bunkers.

Asking himself, 'Now, who is going to win on this terrific course?' Darwin suggested Mitchell and Jones. He was writing before Mitchell fell away in his 72-hole match against Hagen, an experience from which he had not recovered by the time of the Open. Jones was seen by Darwin as having indisputable claims to be in stroke play the first favourite in any field in the world. He pointed out that 'in the American championships since the war (remember that he is, to-day, only twenty-four years old) Mr. Jones is in the aggregate nineteen shots ahead of the next man and that next man is Walter Hagen. I doubt if Vardon himself in his greatest days ever had such a record as that. It speaks for itself.' It is worth bearing in mind that half this period was in what is called Jones's seven lean years.

Darwin predicted that Jones would find St Anne's to his liking: 'Moreover, I think St Anne's should suit him. He has all the length anyone can want. The fact that the bunkers are near the holes should not trouble a player of his arrow-like straightness and besides, as an enthusiastic American exclaimed at Muirfield, "Bobby don't mind traps."'

The long driving competition

Although of no great relevance to the Open that was to follow, the long driving championship, held on the day before the first round at Lytham & St Anne's, gives a fascinating insight into the performance of the clubs and balls of the time.

The marked-out area referred to is likely to have been on what was then called 'The Ladies' Course'. It is known from an aerial photograph in the 1930s that several par-four holes ran up and down what is now the practice ground.

The account given in *The Times* of the long driving event indicates that the wind was from left to right and the ground soft. The distances achieved must therefore have been nearly all carry. They compare very favourably with those realised by the modern clubs and balls of today.

Darwin's writing remains as delicate and delightful as ever. It warrants reproduction in full:

All the great men of the earth are now assembled at St. Anne's for the Championship, which will be begun to-day. Yesterday the long driving competition for the Field Cup acted as an aperitif before the serious feast. The similitude is not inappropriate for, as with cocktails so with this long driving competition, a little of it is extremely cheering, but you must not have too much. Though it is exceedingly well organised, there is a certain amount of waiting and, after you have watched for some time, you suddenly feel that you want to do something else.

The conditions yesterday were decidedly interesting, for a very strong westerly wind was blowing off the drivers' backs, and inevitably anything in the nature of a slice was out of bounds. In the circumstances the majority of the onlookers congregated continuously on the left of the staked course, and only a few intrepid ones, hoping perhaps to recapture the sensations of an air raid, stood on the right. The fairway could hardly have been better, being dead flat, rather slow, and of an even consistency, so that the chance of a lucky fall on hard ground was reduced to a minimum. At 2 o'clock Sir Theodore Cook waved his white flag from the starting-point, but it was not until half an hour later that the recognised sloggers began to appear on the tee. The first of them was Curtis, of Bournemouth, who at once set up an aggregate of 790 yards for the best three drives out of four, which gave other people something to beat. Curtis is a tall man who stands well up to his ball with his arms noticeably close to his side. As he addresses the ball he looks a little 'tucked up', but there is nothing cramped about his hitting.

After Curtis came a short interval of dullness, the telegraph board clanked dismally like a skeleton in chains, and the clouds were black and the wind blew chill, but then the magic name Tolley was announced, 'and the great Lord of Luna comes with his stately stride.' Everybody cheered up and Mr. Tolley began with a beauty, starting out to the left and swinging in with the wind. Alas, the next was out of bounds, and the next also, up went the black flag, and we had a gruesome feeling of waiting outside Pentonville. This meant that Mr. Tolley's chances of the aggregate prize were gone, but he might still win that for the best shot. Involuntarily the spectators cowered before the last blow, and a very fine one it was, 275 yards, beating Curtis's best shot by three yards. Almost immediately after came Jack Smith, of Wentworth, who has won this competition twice before. His first two were lovely shots; he took it noticeably easily yet, even so, the club sang through the air; the third was heeled and was out of bounds; the fourth was a gallant effort, but not quite long enough, and Smith's aggregate was seven yards behind Curtis and his best shot four yards behind Mr. Tolley.

Next came Bingham, another mighty slasher, but he was a little disappointing. Boomer then hit some very fine shots without disturbing either of the leaders, though he passed Smith, and then came the Argentine player, Jurado. Of all the drivers he gave the most favourable impression of hitting hard, for you could see the club quivering at the end of the shot. His first drive was 279 yards, and he waved his hands over his head with joy and bowed gracefully to the cheers that greeted him. Sad to say, the very next shot, by Havers, beat him by 7 inches. Havers's first two shots were so very fine that he seemed to have the aggregate prize also in his grasp. But his third was too much held up and his fourth was quite short, so that Curtis could breathe again. Duncan hit three beautiful shots, winded to perfection, and then I began to feel as if I were watching Rhodes Scholars pole-jumping at Queen's Club on a raw afternoon in March. I confess that I deserted my post, but the drivers went on driving and driving and the white and black flags waved. The figures must tell the story how Compston, with a best shot of 288 yards, beat the unlucky Curtis's aggregate by three inches.

If only the same wind blows to-day there will be some intensely interesting golf, for the bunkers round the greens are like the troops of Midian in the hymn, they are bound to catch the most accurate. In fact, in watching a few holes yesterday I saw more illustrious persons delving in sand than I have seen for a long time, and a most cheering spectacle it was.

The leading returns were:

Aggregate (best three of four balls)
A. Compston (unattached), 790 yd. 0ft. 7in
D.A. Curtis (Queen's Park, Bournemouth), 790 yd. 0ft. 4in.
A. Boomer (St. Cloud, Paris), 788 yd. 1ft. 7in.
J. Smith (Wentworth), 783 yd. 1ft. 4in.
Mr. R. Mackenzie (USA), 780 yd. 1ft. 11in.
A.G. Havers (Coombe Hill), 772 yd. 1ft. 8in.
G. Duncan (Wentworth), 756 yd. 1ft. 9in.
F. Rutter (Neasden), 750 yd. 2ft. 1in.

Single (best one of four drives)
Compston, 288 yd. 0ft. 3in
Havers, 279 yd. 0ft. 10in.
J. Jurado, (Argentina), 279 yd. 0ft. 3in.
Mr. C.J.H. Tolley (Rye), 275 yd. 1ft. 1in.
J. Stein (USA), 275 yd.
Smith, 272 yd. 1ft. 4in.
Curtis, 272 yd. 0ft. 8in.
Boomer, 268 yd. 1ft. 9in.
Mr. Mackenzie, 267 yd. 2ft. 5in.
A. Easterbrook (Sidmouth), 265 yd. 2ft.
Rutter, 262 yd. 1ft. 1in.
R.A. Whitcombe, 260 yd. 2ft. 2in.
Duncan, 255 yd. 1ft. 1in.

The long driving competition was a distraction that gave thrills to the onlookers but no guide as to who might win.

Indeed it is worth noting that the event was avoided by most of big names and in particular neither Jones nor Hagen allowed their concentration to be broken by taking part in the diversion. They had a more important matter awaiting them the next morning.

CHAPTER TEN

Meet the players

The British Open Championship of 1926 took place nearly ninety years ago. To set the scene, it may therefore be helpful to have glimpses of the players other than Jones.

Even without Jones, the 1920s was a strong decade for American golf. Walter Hagen, Gene Sarazen, Tommy Armour and Leo Diegel headed the professional game and Chick Evans, Francis Ouimet and George Von Elm the amateur.

Walter Hagen

While Walter Hagen and Bobby Jones differed in so many ways, each liked the other and they enjoyed playing together. Jones said, 'I love playing with Walter. He goes along, chin up, smiling away; never grousing about his luck, playing the ball as he finds it. He can come nearer beating the luck than anyone else I know.' Hagen was the ultimate one-off and his efforts transformed the lives and prospects of his fellow professionals. They would not even consider imitating his way of life, but appreciated the beneficial impact he made on theirs.

In his first appearance in the British Open in 1920 at Deal he started brightly in the first round, going out in 37 strokes before an abject back nine of 48 gave him a miserable 85. To this he added a second round of 84 and finished in 55th place. Being Hagen, he had played the last few holes with great concentration and deliberation. When asked why, he replied, 'I was scared I might finish 56th!' before adding, 'I'll be back.' He did return, finishing sixth at St Andrews in 1921 before winning his first Open in 1922 at Sandwich.

It was at Deal that he struck some early blows for the downtrodden professionals. His trip was financed by a Detroit millionaire and 'The Haig' arrived with four trunks full of clothes. He was denied access to the clubhouse for changing, instead being offered a nail on the wall in the professional's shop. His solution was to have his chauffeur park his long, luxurious Daimler in front of the clubhouse, using it as his own locker room and changing his shoes on the running board. Also denied access to the clubhouse for his meals, he hired an airplane and every day arranged to be flown with his companions to a reputable restaurant, telling officials he preferred the strawberries there.

The following year he was denied access to the clubhouse to change at Troon, but on completion of the event he was invited by the secretary to enter the clubhouse for the presentation. Instead he made his way through the crowd to the door and then turned to tell those gathered that rather than go into the clubhouse now, he would go to a nearby pub where he and the other players had been made welcome all week.

He was one of the first sportsmen to make a million dollars, but he spent it faster than he made it. Spurning the life of a club professional, he would play an exhibition wherever a crowd could be assembled. A week after returning to San Francisco from a tour of exhibitions that had generated $23,000 for him (although the associated expenses had been greater than the income) he had been compelled to stay in his hotel room for several days, unable to pay for his laundry. He famously said, 'I never wanted to be a millionaire, I just wanted to live like one.'

Often his solution to a crisis was the big gesture. After winning his fourth and last British Open in 1929, he returned completely broke to New York. Borrowing the $25 his son had won the previous day, he used that money for a taxi to the Delmonico hotel. Instead of taking his usual suite, he asked for an entire floor. He then asked the front desk to send up $500 in new twenties and add that amount to his bill. Finally he called his agent Bob Harlow, telling him to book a few exhibitions urgently.

Due to play Mike Brady in a play-off for the 1919 US Open at Brae Burn, Hagen's preparation was to go to a party, meet a young lady, take her to see the show *Sinbad the Sailor* in Boston and then join the star of the show Al Jolson in his hotel suite until the early hours. Walter arose after three hours' sleep and won the play-off with a hangover.

The way he marked his first British Open win was entirely in character. He accepted his winner's cheque, then gave it to his caddie as a tip, before travelling to Southampton in a rented Rolls-Royce and sailing back across the Atlantic in a first-class cabin.

Between 1914 and 1932 he won eleven majors. Despite the presence of Jones, he won two US Opens, four British Opens and also won the USPGA five times. The Western Open was regarded as a major at that time and he had five wins in that event. He played in the first five Ryder Cups between 1927 and 1935.

His approach to life was delightfully summed up by his saying: 'Don't hurry, don't worry, you're only here for a short visit, so be sure to smell the flowers along the way.'

Al Watrous

Al Watrous had been raised in Yonkers, New York and had come up through the ranks as a caddie. For a while he had caddied for Hagen. After a spell in the US Navy, he moved to Detroit, taking up a position as assistant club professional. He was an accomplished player, winning the Canadian Open at the age of 23. He was something of a home bird, spending his life in Michigan and subsequently succeeding Hagen as head professional at Oakland Hills Country Club.

The life of a touring pro held little appeal for him but in 1926 Hagen told the members of Grand Rapids that they should let their assistant have a go at the British Open and an entry was posted for what was for Watrous his first trip across the Atlantic. Many were impressed with the style and ability he showed when he ran Jones so close at St Anne's. His second trip to Britain was as a member of the 1929 Ryder Cup team that lost by seven matches to five at Moortown. In the singles Watrous was out in the last but one match and lost by 4 & 3 to the 22-year-old Henry Cotton. Two years earlier he had played in the first Ryder Cup at Worcester, Massachusetts, winning his foursomes in partnership with Gene Sarazen, and also his singles by 3 & 2 against Fred Robson.

It was to be another 25 years before his third British expedition. In 1954, then aged 55, he received the gift of a trip from the members of his Birmingham Country Club, Michigan with an entry for the British Open being played at Royal Birkdale. He played in the qualifying rounds and had a fine 73 at Hillside in the first round. The *New York Times* noted that 'by quirk of chance he was drawn with A.J. Isherwood of Britain, with whom he had played in the qualifying round twenty-eight years ago.'

Although he shunned the life of a touring professional golfer, the merit and ability he showed at St Anne's remained with him. Staying as he did in Michigan, he was to win the Michigan Open and PGA championships a total of fourteen times. He was popular with his fellow players when he did, on rare occasions, venture away from home. As well as playing in the first two Ryder Cups, he also played in the Masters nine times between 1935 and 1946, finishing seventh in 1937.

His wife bore him five children and other players would tease him, asking, 'How many children have you got now, Al?' Sometimes he answered, 'I don't know. I haven't been home in six weeks.' On other occasions his response was, 'I haven't been out on the front porch to see how many bottles of milk we get each morning.'

He acted as pall-bearer at Walter Hagen's funeral.

George Von Elm

By reaching the final of the 1924 US Amateur, George Von Elm was the first finalist ever to come from west of the Mississippi. Finalist in that year and semi-finalist the following year, his pedigree was obvious.

When it came to the final of the 1926 US Amateur, Jones reached the final in a wearied state, after his victories in the British Open and the US Open. His opponent was once again Von Elm, who in the third round had beaten Watts Gunn comprehensively by 8 & 7. Jones knew that his earlier victories over Von Elm by 9 & 8 in the final of the 1924 US Amateur at Merion (the second highest winning margin in the history of the event) and by 7 & 6 in the 1925 US Amateur at Oakmont counted for little. As he said to Keeler, 'nobody is going to keep on beating a golfer as good as George Von Elm.' In a hard-fought, high-quality final, Von Elm emerged winner by a margin of 2 & 1. It was the first time the trophy had been taken to California and it was the last time anyone beat Jones over 36 holes. One paper commented that 'The Monarch of golf was toppled from his throne by the flaxen haired George Von Elm in one of the most stunning upsets in links history.'

The 1926 Walker Cup was the closest contest of the early years, the USA winning by six-and-a-half matches to five-and-a-half. The match hinged on the struggle between the massive figure of Major Hezlet and George Von Elm. The game was halved and the USA won the match.

Von Elm felt that the adulation showered upon Jones meant people thought less of his golf and he developed an unfortunate antipathy towards Jones over the years. He resented the income Jones was able to receive for his writings while still retaining his amateur status. Von Elm once admitted to golf writer Lester Rice that he 'hated Jones's guts.' Jones was aware of his rival's feelings and said that Von Elm 'always impressed me as having a chip on either shoulder.'

In the 1928 US Open, Von Elm, still an amateur, finished tied in fourth place with Hagen. He also played in the 1928 and 1930 Walker Cups. He turned professional in 1930 with a somewhat bitter letter to the Press. The following year he took a two-shot lead into the final round of the US Open but slipped to a 75 and found himself in a remarkable play-off with Billy Burke. It was by some margin the longest in tournament history. At that time the standard play-off was 36 holes and Von Elm thought he was home. He was – until Burke holed a birdie putt on the last green to tie on 149 strokes. After a further 36 holes, Burke won by one stroke. They had played 144 holes in the one event. Von Elm won the South California Open in 1936.

Tommy Armour

In the First World War Tommy Armour left his studies at the University of Edinburgh to become a machine gunner in the Tank Corps. It is said that he once captured a German tank single-handedly and, his gun having jammed, he climbed out of his tank and strangled a German officer with his bare hands. He lost the sight of one eye at Ypres and shattered his left arm in another battle.

Moving to the United States, he became one of the leading professionals and won the US Open in 1927, the USPGA in 1930 and the British Open in 1931. In the winters of 1925/26 and 1926/27 Armour and Jones played each other many times, Armour admiring the young Georgian's rhythm, timing and concentration and Jones admiring the Scot's iron play and competitiveness. Their matches were intensely fought with barely a word exchanged until after the last putt. Each brought on the other's game. Perhaps more importantly, Armour revealed to the young Jones the mysteries and joys of the Old Course at St Andrews and was largely responsible for transforming the attitude Jones thereafter had for the Old Lady.

Of their matches, Armour lost several before finally accepting one up a side in their bets. When asked years later how he could accept shots from an amateur, the Silver Scot's growled reply was, 'Because that's how goddam good he was.'

The high regard Armour had for Jones both as a golfer and as a man was revealed in an article he penned for *The American Golfer* in 1935 – extracts from this article appear in appendix D.

Watts Gunn

In the 1925 US Amateur at the intimidating Oakmont course, Watts Gunn set a record that it can be said with certainty will never be equalled. After eleven holes of his 36-hole match against Pennsylvania's champion Vincent Bradford, Watts found himself three down. He then won fifteen consecutive holes against his hapless opponent, going on to win by 12 & 10. In the next round, he went on to knock out the former champion Jess Sweetser, by a margin of 11 & 10, winning seventeen holes, halving twelve and losing only two. It was the heaviest defeat Sweetser had in his career. After the match Jones asked Gunn to tell him about it. Gunn had little memory of how the game had progressed, with his recollection of the holes jumbled together. Keeler also asked him how he felt and Gunn, with a dreamy faraway look in his eyes, said, 'Gee, I'm awful hungry. I'm so hungry my pants are about to fall off.'

After winning his semi-final, Gunn had to play his mentor Jones in the final. The evening before, Jones ran into Gunn in the hotel foyer, slipping off to meet a girl he had flirted with earlier that day. Jones turned him round and marched him back to his room, lest Gunn might blame a defeat on other factors. As it turned out, Gunn played well before finally having to bend the knee. It was the first and last time that two players from the same club met in the final.

In 1926 Gunn was in the Walker Cup team for the 1926 match at St Andrews. In the foursomes he partnered Jones against the redoubtable Cyril Tolley and Andrew Jamieson. The latter achieved a famous victory over Bobby Jones in the 1926 British Amateur at Muirfield. At the thirteenth, Gunn holed an unlikely putt measured at 120 feet for a birdie.

The way the Road Hole was played in the Walker Cup lurched from drama to tragedy before finishing in a certain amount of comedy. Tolley and Jamieson found themselves actually on the road after five shots, having pushed the first tee shot out of bounds. Gunn's drive had found the fairway and Jones took the sensible option of a cautious brassie shot to just short of the green. The Americans looked certain to win the hole until Gunn shanked his little pitch and their ball ended up on the road, now having played three. Jamieson played a good recovery shot to within twelve feet of the hole, the Brits' sixth shot.

Now Jones and Gunn had a dilemma. Should Jones play towards the flag, a shot a little over-cooked could end up in Road bunker and anything could happen from there. After much discussion, Jones played his shot off the tarmac back down the seventeenth fairway, away from the green. The calculation was that from there, a pitch and two putts would give them a seven and thereby a half if Tolley were to hole his putt. The American seven was achieved and when Tolley missed the putt, the hole was won, but as Jones commented, 'not until we had used up all our shots and most of the little brains we had.'

Wild Bill Melhorn

Although he won twenty times on the US tour, Bill Melhorn never won a major championship despite finishing on fourteen occasions in the top ten. The closest he came was when he reached the final of the USPGA, then a match play event, only to run up against Walter Hagen. Melhorn's putting tended to let him down under pressure. He led after three rounds in the 1922 US Open, was tied for the lead after three rounds in the 1923 US Open and tied for the lead after the second round in the 1924 US Open. He eventually finished third in the latter event, after Jones had a birdie at the last hole to take second place and Cyril Walker's last round in dreadful conditions carried him past all the others to leave him as the surprise winner.

After his strong showing in the British Open at St Anne's, Melhorn maintained his form in the US Open at Scioto. He led after his first-round 68 and still held the halfway lead at 143 shots, six ahead of eventual winner Jones, before falling away on the last day. Melhorn played in the first Ryder Cup in 1927 and the first Masters in 1934. He expressed his dismay at being omitted from the 1929 Ryder Cup team, which was to lose at Moortown, Yorkshire. His nickname of 'Wild Bill', coined by Leo Diegel, did not refer to problems with his temperament, nor to erratic shots, but came from his tendency to go on a wild spree of low scoring. He often played wearing a cowboy hat. His surname was usually spelt as Melhorn, though in later articles it sometimes appeared as Mehlhorn.

During a round he was inclined to express his displeasure at the outcome of a full shot by snapping the hickory-shafted club over his knee, tossing the fragments aside and striding off after the ball. His main anger was reserved for the greens and he is believed to have been the first golfer to tie his putter to his back bumper so that it might be justly punished on the drive home.

Fred McLeod

Born in Scotland in 1882, the 5' 4" Fred McLeod found himself before the Bench in the Burgh Court at the age of sixteen, charged with the heinous crime of 'Wheeling hand barrow on foot path.' The sentence was 'Dismissed with admonition.' He emigrated to America in 1903 to become a golf professional. Within a few weeks of landing he had played in the US Open. A few weeks later he finished fifth, tied with his old school friend Willie Anderson, in the Western Open, which was at that time a leading event. Over the next few years, he tied for third with Anderson in 1906 and tied for second with him in 1907. In 1908 Anderson won the Western Open by one shot from McLeod. A few weeks later the tables were turned.

At the beginning of the 1908 US Open at Myopia Hunt Club, McLeod weighed 118 pounds. When he lifted the trophy after a play-off with Willie Smith, he weighed 108 pounds, thus becoming the lightest ever winner. In both 1910 and 1911 US Opens he missed out on getting into the play-off by just one shot. In 1919 he finished one shot behind Jim Barnes in the US PGA, and in the 1921 US Open he tied with Hagen for second place, some way behind runaway winner Barnes.

In the British Open at St Anne's in 1926 he was to finish in seventh place.

Frederick J. Wright

In the qualifying rounds of the 1920 US Amateur at the Engineers Club, Freddie Wright tied with Jones for the medal for leading qualifier. They were of the same age and met in the third round in an exceptional match, both seeming to be determined to complete as many holes as possible in three strokes. Wright had a three at the first, Jones at the second, Wright at the fourth. Jones then had threes at the sixth, seventh and eighth. Wright completed the first nine in 35 strokes and found himself two down. Overall Jones had eight threes in his morning round and closed Wright out by 5 & 4.

Wright played in the 1921 match versus Great Britain at Hoylake that was the forerunner of the Walker Cup, and in the 1923 Walker Cup match at St Andrews. In the 1921 British Amateur, the first in which Jones competed, Wright beat Hoylake legend John Ball in an early round. He went further than any other players who made up the American invasion, before losing in the sixth round to the golf writer Bernard Darwin on the nineteenth hole. Darwin was fortunate when his topped shot ran forever on the scorched links at the last hole to edge home against Wright, whose three-hole lead was blown away in the high winds.

Jim Barnes

Born in Cornwall, England, Jim Barnes emigrated to the United States in 1906 and by 1916 was established as a fine player. Unusually tall for that time at 6′ 4″ and nicknamed 'Long Jim', he won the Western Open in 1914. The *New York Times* commented that 'All Barnes needs to win a golf tournament is a good golf course, a putter and a liberal supply of the clover leaves that he carries in the corner of his mouth.' He won the first two PGA Championships played on either side of the First World War in 1916 and 1919. It was in 1919 that he tied for second place in the Canadian Open with Karl Keffer and the seventeen-year-old Bobby Jones. The three of them were an extraordinary sixteen shots behind the winner, Douglas Edgar. In 1919 Barnes won the Southern Open, pushing Jones into second place by playing some exceptional golf.

Barnes became the only US Open winner to be presented with the cup by a current US President in 1921 when Warren G. Harding, who turned up to watch, asked the USGA if he could present the cup, and did. The winning margin of nine strokes remained a record for 80 years. In the 1922 US Open he led after the first round but was overtaken by the winner Gene Sarazen.

Johnnie Farrell

Johnnie Farrell was a tidy dresser, being voted for a number of years the best-dressed golfer on tour and earning the nickname the 'beautiful Irishman'. As a golfer, he was no slouch and had a steely mental side to his game. He was used to winning, having won six consecutive professional tournaments in 1927, a record that was to stand until Byron Nelson's run in 1945. It was in that year that he first ran up against Jones in the early spring in the Southern Open. Jones won that tournament, finishing a remarkable eight shots clear of second-placed Farrell.

Farrell was a worthy winner of the 1928 US Open when he surprised some by beating Jones in the 36-hole play-off, at a time when Jones was at the peak of his game. In the

Plate 1. Mr R.T. Jones by J.A.A. Berrie.

Plate 2. Wild Bill Melhorn and Bobby Jones, complete with cigarette holder.

Plate 3. Mr George Von Elm, who finished in third place, equal with Hagen.

Plate 4. The unique and irrepressible Walter Hagen.

Plate 5. Tom Barber of Cavendish, who finished tied with Abe Mitchell as leading British player in fifth place.

Plate 6. Jones driving, watched by hatted spectators.

Plate 7. Jones putting at the old thirteenth green, now the fourteenth. Note the absence of houses.

Plate 8. Wild Bill Melhorn tee shot at a short hole, probably the fifth.

Plate 9. Hagen's tee shot to the fifteenth in the third round on the final day.

Plate 10. Jones and Al Watrous leave the first tee in the final round.

Plate 11. Watrous drives at the third hole in the final round. Note the large areas of exposed sand in the background.

Plate 12. Jones tees off at a short hole on the final day, watched by his caddie Jack McIntire.

Plate 13. Crowd control, 1926 style – the gallery follow Watrous and Jones down the sixth hole in the final round.

Plate 14. Jones plays a pitch to the sixth green. Note the height to which bunkers are raised above the level of the fourteenth fairway in the background and the extensive area stripped of turf down the right side of that hole.

Plate 15. Watrous watches Jones play to the seventh green. Caddie McIntire has the famous putter 'Calamity Jane' ready.

Plate 16. Jones, seated, watches the first Watrous putt on the seventh green.

Plate 17. The first wobble by Watrous, at the tenth hole in the final round.

Plate 18. The final green. The bunker behind the green was found by Hagen
as he played his last hole.

Plate 19. Jones, having come close to finding the bunker behind the last green, plays his penultimate stroke.

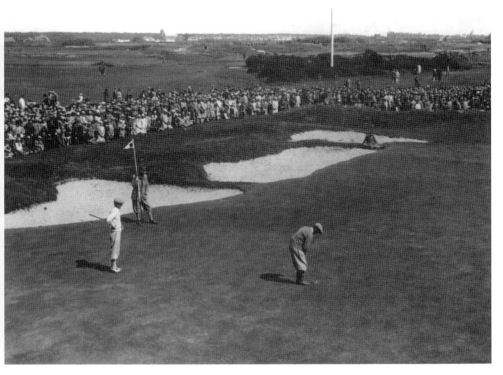

Plate 20. The final putt.

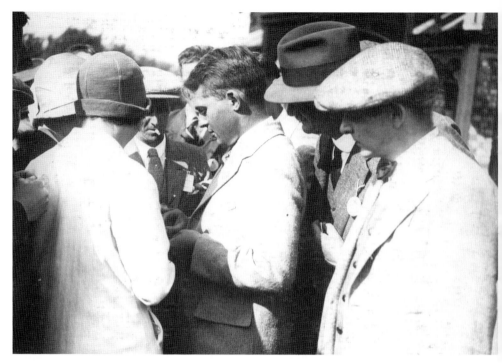

Plate 21. Awaiting the presentation ceremony, the winner signs autographs.

Plate 22. Hagen presents a nonplussed Jones with an outsized niblick.

Plate 23. Jones makes his acceptance speech.

Plate 24. Jones with Norman Boase (left), Chairman on the R&A Championship Committee and a cheerful Hagen behind.

Plate 25. Hero worship after the presentation, including eleven helmeted policemen (or 'bobbies').

Plate 26. The exhausted champion.

Plate 27. The photograph submitted to Jones in 1958 asking whether this was the wonder shot at the penultimate hole (see chapter 17).

Plate 28. Another photograph, of exactly the same shot (in chapter 17 this is shown to have been played at the fourteenth hole in the third round).

Plate 29. The plaque created at the suggestion of Henry Cotton to mark the spot from where the 'immortal shot' was played. It was the world's first such plaque on a golf course.

Plate 30. Jones in USAAF uniform before the Berrie portrait in the clubhouse.

play-off, Farrell finished the morning round with three straight birdies for a three-shot lead over Jones. In the afternoon round, Jones not only made up the deficit but led after the twelfth hole. Farrell birdied the thirteenth to square matters and was one ahead with two to play. At the seventeenth, Farrell was four feet away in two and entitled to feel upbeat until Jones holed from thirty feet to make a birdie of his own. Farrell holed his own putt under immense pressure. When Jones birdied the last, Farrell then holed his own ten-foot putt for another birdie and a one-shot winning margin.

In 1929 Farrell finished runner-up to Walter Hagen in the British Open at Muirfield.

Cyril Walker

Born in Manchester, England, Cyril Walker emigrated to the United States in 1914. Small like Freddie Wright, he only weighed 118 pounds. In the 1924 US Open Jones finished second at Oakland Hills in a howling wind behind Walker, described by Charles Price as 'a pint-sized misanthrope.' The purse for winning was $500. Price goes on to describe how the announcer on the first tee at the Los Angeles Open some six months later 'had got into the habit of thinking Jones was always national champion. Turning aside from the microphone, he asked Walker if he were champion of anything; say, some state. "State" screamed Walker, who was justifiably proud that he had trounced Jones. "I'm champion of the whole goddam forty-eight!"'

Subsequently he was lured into taking on Walter Hagen, then the British Open champion, in a 72-hole match for the unofficial title of champion of the world. Walker was obliterated by a margin of 17 & 15. While this helped Hagen's image, it did little for Walker, the match being described as 'an exhibition of class against mediocrity.' Nothing however should detract from Walker's heroic play of the last nine holes in appalling weather to become the 1924 US Open champion. Jones, who finished alone in second place three shots behind, said, 'This guy is good. He can shoot a game of golf and won by shooting a damnsite [*sic*] better than anyone else in the show. Naturally I am disappointed at not retaining my title, but I have no excuse to offer and no complaints to make.' This generous statement was considered to 'epitomize the American ideal of sportsmanship.'

Archie Compston

By 1926 Archie Compston was an established match player but his stroke play record before and after was far from shoddy. He had some good finishes in the British Open, tied for ninth in 1920, tied for second behind Jim Barnes at Prestwick in 1925 and finished third behind Hagen at Sandwich in 1928. After 54 holes in the 1930 Open at Hoylake, he stood on the brink of destroying Jones's hopes of winning the Grand Slam. His stunning third round of 68 had swept him past Jones and into the lead, but in the afternoon he fell to pieces with an 82 and tied for sixth.

In his first of two appearances in the US Open he finished a commendable tied seventh in 1927 and tied 22nd in 1928.

He made three Ryder Cup appearances in 1927, 1929 and 1931. In the 1929 match at Moortown near Leeds, he beat Gene Sarazen by 6 & 4 in a 36-hole match.

He had the unusual custom of taking out three caddies, the first to carry his clubs, the second to carry his apparel and the third his cigarettes, cigars and pipes as he smoked his way around the course.

An insight into his perception of golf as a game is given by his saying, 'Next to sunburn, a visit to the dentist, or a wasp sting on the privates, nothing gives a man more masochistic satisfaction than a round of golf.' He was for some time personal golf tutor to the Prince of Wales, thereafter briefly King Edward VII.

In the run-up to the 1928 British Open, Compston threw down a challenge to Hagen over 72 holes at Moor Park, which was readily accepted. The British player won by the remarkable margin of 18 & 17. After the match Hagen said to the assembled crowds, 'When you're laid out good and flat, you mustn't squawk!' Hagen's manager Bob Harlow was distraught as he saw the planned earnings for the imminent tour evaporating before his eyes. Hagen was unperturbed. As the two drove away from the venue, Walter was in thoughtful mood. He drew deeply on his cigarette and, as he exhaled, said, 'You know, I can beat that son-of-a-bitch any day of the week.' Two weeks later at Sandwich in the British Open, it was Hagen first, Sarazen second, and Compston third.

J.A.A. Berrie, whose painting of Bobby Jones (see plate 1) hangs in the clubhouse at St Anne's, also produced a painting of Compston, which is in the Harrogate Museum, Yorkshire.

Tom Barber

Tom Barber took up the position of professional at Alderley Edge in 1922 and the following year qualified for the match play stages of the Yorkshire Evening News tournament at Headingley Golf Club. He found himself in a field that included Gene Sarazen and Walter Hagen, both warming up for the British Open at Troon. In the first round Barber was drawn against Hagen and came close to creating a major upset. After Barber won the eighteenth hole to square the match, it was only at the 21st that Hagen scraped home. To do so he had to negotiate a good stymie by chipping over Barber's ball into the hole.

Barber reached the semi-final of the News of the World Matchplay in 1924 and the following year he moved to Cavendish, Derbyshire. He was to finish a good fifth to Jones at St Anne's in 1926 and in 1931 only lost at the 39th hole to Charles Whitcombe in the final of the Yorkshire Evening News event. He moved to Royal Zoute in Belgium, where he died suddenly in 1936. His surname is at times spelled Barbour.

Cyril Tolley

'Tolley the Magnificent', as he was sometimes called, was a great example of the true amateur golfer. Endued with great talent, he played with élan and joy. He was a contemporary at Oxford of another Corinthian, Roger Wethered, who was inclined to pass up a play-off for the 1921 British Open because he had promised to play in a cricket match that day.

Tolley was above all a match player, winning the British Amateur twice in 1920 and 1929, the French Amateur twice (one suspects he travelled more for the wine than the golf), and the Welsh Amateur twice, also playing in five Walker Cups. His ethos was revealed when decrying cautious play. 'Far better to take a risk and fail to make a Herculean recovery and then try to hole the putt,' he said, 'than to go on mechanically playing a dull, uneventful game at that youthful age.'

The flavour of the man is revealed in an article in the *Oxford Times*:

Cyril Tolley (1895–1978) … came up to University College in 1919 at the age of 24, long after leaving Westminster School. He had already been awarded the MC during service in the Royal Tank Corps for leading his tank on foot during the battle of Cambrai.

Liddell Hart called Cambrai 'one of the landmarks in the history of warfare, the dawn of a new epoch' as it demonstrated, at last, how the Hindenburg line could be penetrated, although it might have been more safely done from inside the tank. Tolley himself was taken prisoner and forced to sit out the rest of the action.

Coming up to Oxford five years later than he might have done, Tolley wasted little time in making his mark on the place, quite literally if a report in *Time Magazine* (September 29, 1924) is to be believed: 'Since he first hove into the public eye, Tolley has been touted as a merry, garrulous, quip-cracking links-wit. Tales are told of his Oxford days when, in postprandial exuberance, he would harangue a blithe gathering in his rooms upon his years of study at the science of propelling a spheroid. He would then tee a ball on the carpet and drive it smashing through a closet panel.

'Another feat was to loft balls from the lawn of University College to the sward of Queen's College over the walls and across the High Street. A servant would then call at Queens, asking politely: "Mr. Tolley's compliments to the gentlemen of Queens and might he have his golf balls back?"' If a jigger would have sufficed to reach the pristine lawns of Queen's, I imagine a full mashie niblick would have been needed to interrupt the reveries of All Soul's.

… After skipping lectures and dusting off his playing skills at Frilford, he entered for the British Amateur Championship of 1920 at Muirfield. Today the Amateur is a bit of a sideshow, but in 1920 it was one of the most prestigious of all sporting events. In typically swashbuckling style, Tolley made it through to the 36-hole final against the experienced American, Robert Gardner. But the chain-smoking English underdog in the tweed plus-fours and old school tie triumphed with a long putt at the first play-off hole.

Tolley's Muirfield triumph is eloquently described in *Some Batsmen and Bowlers (1920–1940)* (Sportsman's Book Club, 1943) by R.C. Robertson-Glasgow, the John Arlott of his day: 'Everyone that evening in the streets of Oxford seemed to be reading the stop press as each breathless edition came out. Tolley sent false news of his time of return but the men of University College met every train, and, making their kill at last, removed a horse and dragged the champion round the city in an ancient Victoria.'

Tolley and Jones enjoyed each other's approach to golf and life. The evening before the singles in the 1926 Walker Cup, played over the Old Course at St Andrews, Jess Sweetser was talking to Bobby Jones and mentioned his concern about Jones's opponent the next day, Cyril Tolley, and his prodigious driving ability. Jones replied, 'Jess, don't you worry about Tolley.' The following morning Tolley hit a splendid drive some 275 yards and, without any obvious effort, Jones passed him by 25 yards. The same happened at the second hole. Thereafter Tolley was striving for unnecessary length. The result of the 36-hole match was that Jones won by 12 & 11.

CHAPTER ELEVEN

The first day

After returning from Sunningdale to St Anne's, Jones continued to practise but he sensed that the magic of that first qualifying round was leaving him.

The weather for the first round was ideal for golf, fine with at times a fresh, strong north-westerly breeze helping the players on the front nine but making the journey home attritional. Early in the day it became clear that the Americans were scoring impressively and the hoped-for British challenge was not happening. By the end of the day, American players were to occupy the first five places.

Of the earlier American starters, Tommy Armour's long game was impressive but his putting fragile. In the first few holes he left himself missable putts but managed to slide them in until the fifth hole, where he was rattled after three-putting. The *Scotsman* recalled that in the past Armour had run out of patience with various putters and on the return train journey after one event had jettisoned a considerable number of putters from the railway carriage window. Here at St Anne's he missed short putts at three holes around the turn and had to settle for a 74. As the *New York Times* noted, 'He was ill at ease and nervous on the greens, and nervousness on the greens cannot be hidden any more than a red nose can.'

Fred McLeod was originally from North Berwick but after 25 years in the United States was now an American player, having won the US Open in 1908. He showed that good putting was possible. The *Scotsman* described his work on the greens as 'some of the most astonishing putting ever seen in a championship. When McLeod's putter touched the ball it went away as if taken by an electric current straight to the hole, not every time of course, but eight times in the round.' At the sixth, he holed from twelve yards for a par, at the ninth from eight yards for a two and at the sixteenth from eight yards again for a birdie three. Two sixes and another dropped shot at the fourteenth meant he had to settle for a 71. This meant a share of eventual third place with his playing partner, the young American Al Watrous, who got a five at the seventeenth despite being in three bunkers. Darwin 'had doubts whether McLeod can quite go the pace, good as he is' but liked what he saw of Watrous, who 'is one of the best of the younger Americans, with a fine free and yet leisurely style.' Watrous, Darwin pointed out, 'has youth on his side and must be dangerous.'

The next leading American out was Mr 'Bobby' Jones who, as favourite, attracted a large crowd. From his opening shot at half past eleven, Jones knew he was in for a long struggle. The *New York Times* described him as 'nervous and unsettled at the start.' The par-three first hole measured

223 yards and a necklace of bunkers around the green put pressure on the player from the off. With a long iron, Jones hooked his tee shot wide of the bunkers and his chip cleared the bunker by no more than a few inches, leaving him settling for a four. At the second his driving accuracy left him again and another hook left him in the rough but after a good recovery shot he got his four. Normal service was resumed at the third and he had a holeable birdie opportunity but had to settle for a four.

After a par at the fourth, he hit a weak tee shot to the short fifth, but his precise chip-and-run left him a tap-in for his three. At the 431-yard sixth he was comfortably on in two, but left his first and second putts short. An article in the *Scotsman* noted that after three-putting, 'there was one moment when his temper did out and this wonderful young player showed a touch of the Old Adam ... after missing a four-foot putt, he knocked the ball in, picked it out, and then dashed it on the ground in annoyance. This was very like the petulant Mr. Jones of five years ago, but it is the only peep of this kind I have seen since he came over on the present visit.' Compared this with his earlier outbursts, this has to be seen as commendably restrained.

'He's mad,' said an American spectator to Darwin, who noted that 'though Jones showed no outward sign of anger, yet somehow one felt that he wanted to kick himself.' He got his par five at the 543-yard seventh – what Darwin described as a 'not very good 5' – and after another par four at the eighth, he had his first of a series of struggles with the par-three ninth hole. A pushed tee shot left him a difficult lie in a bunker and after only just getting out, he did well to escape with a four, taking him out in 37 shots. Playing the back nine into the wind, he scored better by coming back in 35.

At the par-four tenth he almost got a three, but at 600 yards into the wind the green at the eleventh was out of reach even for three good full wooden shots. From just short of the green Jones played a superb running chip with a short cleek specially cut down for the purpose, to within two yards and holed the putt. At 313 yards, the short par-four twelfth offered a birdie chance, which Jones accepted after his chip left him a six-foot putt. 'Another drive of 280 yards at the twelfth broke the shell of another egg and a birdie hopped out,' wrote Anthony Spalding whimsically in the *New York Times*. 'Bobby was getting good figures, but they were not coming easily.' At the thirteenth he took his driving iron from the tee but cut the shot badly and emerged with a one-over-par five, being fortunate that his ball avoided being buried in the rushes.

After getting his four at the fourteenth, he pushed his tee shot at the short fifteenth into a bunker and some predicted he was heading for a 74. However, he chipped out well and holed his putt before holing single putts on two of the last three holes. At the last he holed his first putt of any length when a ten-yarder went in for a back nine of 35, the best of the day. He had used 29 putts in the round of 72, which was to leave him on his own in fifth place.

Wild Bill Melhorn was the next American to shine. At the first hole his mashie left him on a bank from where he pitched out to ten feet and holed the putt. At the 423-yard second, after his mashie niblick second shot, he holed a fourteen-yard putt for a three. He missed from five feet at the fifth. At the sixth he had the misfortune to have his ball rest in a deep divot, from which he was only made to move the ball a short distance, and it was only by pitching to within twelve inches of the hole that he was able to get a five. His second shot at the long seventh with a brassie was bunkered, leading to another five. At the ninth he missed from six feet to drop a shot to par.

The eleventh was his finest effort. Other players had been short after three good shots but after Melhorn hit a huge drive – he said, 'I hit it down that fairway a mile' – followed by an equally good brassie for his third shot, he needed only a three-quarter swing with a mashie to leave his ball twenty yards from the hole. He then holed the putt for the only birdie of the day on that hole. After three-putting the sixteenth, Melhorn bounced back with a birdie three at the seventeenth which Darwin described as a 'most difficult dog-legged hole, bristling with trouble.' The round was described as 'the result of sterling work, in which the driving, very long and extremely accurate considering the narrowness of the course, was the feature of his game.'

Melhorn's score of 70 was to leave him in second place at the end of the first day. The *Scotsman* noted that 'an adventurous round it was with some magnificent thrusts, some dangerous neck or nothing situations in it. Mehlhorn is a powerful golfer, with something of the slap-dash and the long stroke in his play and a lot of resource in recovery. Today he drove as few could drive – great raking strokes, particularly against the stiff wind. Wild Bill Mehlhorn had no need to be wild today, and none for snapping a club over his knee, as he has been known to do.'

What of the British players? All were out of the headlines. Abe Mitchell had arrived with the support of many but only managed to complete the first nine in 36 by good fortune. He hooked his brassie shot at the seventh into a bed of stinging nettles growing on a sand dune, from where he was only able to move the ball a few yards and did well to hole out in six. His sliced drive at the eighth ended in heavy rough and he was fortunate to get a four. Against the wind his game fell away and after a seven on the eleventh and a drive into gorse at the eighteenth, he took 42 to come home.

Darwin observed that 'Mitchell, alack! had taken 78. I do not think Mitchell is very well, and I am sure that he is very tired. He has for the moment had too much golf and is like many worthy citizens who would much rather sit in their gardens than put on a black coat and go to the office. As at St George's Hill, in his match with Hagen, Mitchell seems to be losing control of his left hand. There was a lack of firmness there and the ball was too often pushed out to the right instead of being held on the line.'

George Duncan played steadily for a 75 but his putting let him down. He was joined on that score by the great J.H. Taylor, who had for the previous few years been talking about retirement. He is described by the *Scotsman* as an 'old dog for a hard road' who had set out with the old stride and did some excellent placing of the ball where it needed to be placed. Harry Vardon was by this stage some way past his golfing prime. Although on the front nine he pushed back the years and went out in 35 to the delight of many, his game fell to pieces on the back nine and he returned an 80.

The leading British players were the Scottish champion Tom Wilson and Reg Whitcombe on 73. Wilson, though, had wrenched his knee playing a cleek shot on the fifteenth tee and although he manfully finished 3, 4, 3, 4 he was doubtful for the second round. A new system was in operation for this Open in which all players fifteen shots or more behind the leader after two rounds were to be 'compulsorily retired'. This was to give a manageable size of field for the 36 holes to be played on the final day. After the first round, Darwin mentioned this formula and wondered if, after the second round, there would be any British players left in the competition.

The lead after the completion of the opening round was held by none other than the debonair Walter Hagen. His appearance on the first tee was described by the *Scotsman* in some detail:

> There was a little delay about the time he went off this afternoon, and he was the picture of eagerness on the first tee, walking up and down, glancing up to see what progress in front. Swinging his iron, he was straining at the leash to go to it, as they say in America, and a crowd of about two thousand accompanied him. When he did hit off he was bareheaded, with black hair shining above his deeply bronzed features, and with him was the caddie he has specially brought over from America.

The *New York Times* told how on the first tee, 'he paraded around the teeing ground wearing his "diamond and sceptre" look of victory.'

At the second Hagen holed a twelve-yard putt for an early birdie and the *Scotsman* reported that 'by a hair's breadth he missed doing the one putt trick in a phenomenal sequence with the next three greens.' He had a birdie four at the seventh and was out in 32 after golf of the highest calibre. The back nine was a contrast: some good, some fortunate, some based on skilful recovery shots. At the tenth he had a solid birdie three. At the eleventh he was bunkered but with a single putt got his five. At the twelfth it was only because his cut drive struck a lady that he ended on the fringe of a bunker and not buried in it – from where he pitched into another bunker. From there he came out to twelve feet and holed the putt for an unlikely four.

At the thirteenth Hagen topped a cleek along the ground that left him with a full mashie that he put into a bunker. The *New York Times* noted that 'There was another display of fireworks. He topped his second and his pitch went into a bunker in a jolly awkward place. Hagen smiled a smile grim and saturnine, and got down into the bunker, from where he carefully and geographically surveyed the promised land. Then completely unconcerned, he settled down and played. The ball came to rest seven feet from the pin and down it went.' A scrambled five but a shot dropped. At the fourteenth he pulled his tee shot into a bunker. After coming out he ran his chip from fifty yards stone dead for a par four. At the short fifteenth he missed the green by some distance but pitched close and holed his putt.

His play at the sixteenth was straightforward, with a gorgeous drive, pitch and good three-yard putt for a birdie three. Two fours would have given him a 67 but he missed a fairly short putt at the seventeenth. At the last hole he was some way short of the green with his second, but he ran his next shot to five feet from the flag and tapped in for a 68. It was reported in the *Daily Telegraph* that 'his marker shook him warmly by the hand and the crowd applauded in appreciation of a marvellous performance. Another score like this tomorrow and the championship is virtually over.'

Darwin observed that the pace of play by Hagen left something to be desired, commenting that 'Hagen was doing wonderful things. It must be admitted that he did them at rather a funereal pace, for he and his partner Kirby lost four clear holes on the couple in front, and, even allowing for the crowd, this was altogether too much, and was rather hard on those that followed.' Referring to his repeated escapes on the back nine, Darwin commented, 'It was as if a billiards player should think that the spectators had seen enough of nursery cannons, deliberately break up the balls, and show them a little open play as a change.'

'Hagen played with the greatest possible care, leaving nothing to chance. In fact he was so meticulous in this respect that he took three hours to complete the round,' noted journalist George Greenwood. This was viewed as scandalously slow play. Anthony Spalding observed that 'The big crowd that came in with Hagen watched him out of curiosity, but his performance received little applause compared with the compliment paid to Mehlhorn and Bobby Jones. The public has not forgiven him for his failure to turn up punctually for his match against Mitchell.'

There was clearly a coolness if not an antipathy towards Hagen. In part this reflected his conduct in the match against Mitchell but also was an indication that neither Hagen's slow play nor his exuberant character were universally liked. In the club's archives is a letter from Dr Jack Warren to his son Rob, written in 1993 when Jack was in his nineties. Dinner each night was taken at the Majestic Hotel in St Anne's Square:

Dear Rob,

The next time you see Bill Deedes he might be interested to know that your Pa was a guest of the Captain of Lytham St Annes for the whole week of the 1926 Open. I was most priviledged [*sic*] to sit at the Captain's Table and to shake hands with the great young gentleman [Jones]. He was always early to bed and stopped to have a word with the Captain. The most unpopular contestant was Walter Hagen, who kept all those behind waiting, while he walked backwards and forwards, stepping out the distance of his second shot to each hole. He was also living it up on the dance floor into the small hours, the worst type of American! My host that week was a shipping broker named Fairbank. His son was at St Bees and Cambridge with me, of course we all called him Duggie in spite of the missing letter S.

In *Down the Fairway*, written in 1927, Jones looked back at his first round:

I was out in 37, missing the ninth green completely on a pitch downwind, and in order to come home in 35 I used only a single putt on the last four greens – two of 6 feet; one of 10; and the last one of 20. And I should be the last man in the world, I hope, to contend that that is golf.

CHAPTER TWELVE

The second day

If the first day belonged to Hagen, the second day did not belong to anyone. Hagen fell away but no one picked up the torch. However, the American supremacy became even more clearly evident, as by the end of the day they occupied eight of the first ten places. Of the leading British players after the first day, the Scot Tom Wilson's knee injury had not improved overnight and he withdrew. Archie Compston stayed in touch, following his opening 74 with a steady 76.

Once again the day was sunny and although the wind was lighter, the greens became increasingly more slick as the day wore on. Hagen was out at 10.30am, with a 2,000-strong gallery waiting for fireworks. Instead they saw an error-strewn front nine with little sign of the miraculous recoveries of the previous day. On the way out he was in no fewer than six bunkers, in view of which his 38 was commendable. He was pushing many of his shots and was bunkered at the first before visiting two bunkers at the fourth and two bunkers at the seventh, and finally another at the ninth. He was still irritatingly slow. George Greenwood, writing in the *Daily*

Telegraph commented that 'His painstaking and prospecting for invisible hayseeds on the line of the putt became wearisome to spectators and a nuisance to players behind, whose honking left Walter unmoved.'

After pitching to four feet at the tenth, he missed the putt for a birdie. Darwin noted he 'made a downright bad putt, lifting club and body as he hit the ball, which sidled past the hole and a great chance was lost.' Bold shots on the back nine saw him through the green at the fourteenth, fifteenth and seventeenth, dropping shots at two of the holes for a round of 77.

Watching the round, Hagen's wife Margaret insightfully remarked, 'Well, he will have to work all the harder to-morrow.' His pace of play was as unsatisfactory as it had been on the first day. It was noted that 'He took infinite care with his strokes, sizing up the ground, walking up the line of his putts, and in these times of concentration, he just looked at us as if he were not aware of our existence at all.'

After 36 holes, only those players within fifteen shots of the leader would still be in the field, so Hagen's decline was welcome news to many. Greenwood thought that 'Judged by his previous day's standard, Hagen played shockingly. He scrambled round in 77, and was indeed, fortunate not to be several strokes more. But Hagen likes, or pretends he likes to be a stroke behind, because, as he explains, it is a situation which encourages him to fight the harder and with greater determination. "What is one shot," he says, 'when there are two critical rounds to play? Why, one shot is nothing."'

Melhorn went out in an unspectacular 35, but having once again put his third shot on the green at the long eleventh, proceeded to take three putts. At the thirteenth he cut his second shot with a wood into a bunker, from where he went into another bunker and emerged with another six. At the sixteenth he missed a short putt of just two feet. Greenwood noted that this was 'a fact that greatly annoyed him. But he refrained from placing the club across his knee as is his wont with implements that exhibit signs of naughtiness.' He came home in 39 and his second-round 74 put him one ahead of Hagen. Despite having a six at the par-three first and another at the par-four tenth hole, the American amateur George Von Elm added a solid 72 to his first round of 75.

Next out was Jones, accompanied once again by a large crowd, who went out just before one o'clock. Of the 5,000 attending, most seemed to be with Jones and it took five minutes to manage the crowd before many shots. He dropped a shot at the second where he drove into the rough and then visited a bunker. Thereafter, as Darwin observed, 'all was well for a stretch of ten holes, the strokes, save at one hole, the fifth, flowing from his clubs in the very poetry of golf action. He put his second four yards from the pin at the fourth, and the ball, from that delightfully silky putting swing of his, went straight for the hole and down.'

At the next hole, the short fifth, he had an awkward lie in a bunker to the right of the green. Without the aid of the modern sand wedge he played an outstanding explosion shot to within a foot of the hole. He followed this with a four at the sixth and was 34 to the turn. Holeable birdie putts at the eighth and tenth refused to drop, and at the eleventh it looked as though his round might unravel. With the balls and hickory clubs of the time, this hole, at 600 yards into the wind, was proving to be a problem. Cyril Tolley had taken an eleven at the hole earlier in the day.

George Greenwood of the *Daily Telegraph* was with Jones and reported that 'Mr. Jones hooked his drive into the long grass and, taking a brassie, did not get very far, as seemed highly probable from the unpromising lie. But his third, still played with the same club, was one of the most glorious shots I have ever witnessed. Against the wind, the shot must have been 285 yards in length. Mr. Jones was still twenty yards short of the green, and his run up was five or six yards too far. It looked as if he was to register his first 6 of the championship, but down went the putt for a five and he was saved.' He was lucky when a shot running through the back of the seventeenth was stopped by spectators, but he missed from five feet as he had done at the thirteenth a little earlier. He came back in 38 for another round of 72 and tied for the lead with Melhorn on 144. When asked about Hagen, Jones commented that he did not fear Hagen when he was four ahead, but did not like him when four behind.

The previous day, McLeod and Watrous had both had 71s playing together and on the second day the symmetry continued as both had 75s to share fourth place on 146. McLeod dropped three shots at the first three holes but was steady thereafter. An observer noted that 'though he is little he is very good, with a fine stout heart, and is one of the smoothest, sweetest putters you could hope to see.' The 26-year-old Watrous could have had a better score but on the front nine missed twice from five feet and once from two feet. He was a player held in particularly high regard by Hagen, who had encouraged him to cross the Atlantic. Both McLeod and

Watrous were bunkered at the seventeenth, on either side of the green, but each exploded out to six feet and holed the putt for a four. Americans Cyril Walker – who with George Gadd had the low round of the day with 71 – and Tommy Armour were joined on 150 by Archie Compston and Tom Barber of Cavendish, providing the British challenge, such as it was.

The play of the British players failed once again. One paper reported that 'the rout of the British players in the Open championship on the Royal Lytham and St Anne's links, as a result of to-day's play, is complete.' The *New York Times* tangled its metaphors when it noted that 'the British position was fore-shadowed yesterday when 75 per cent of the players seemed to have one foot in the grave and the other on a banana skin.' Mitchell looked exhausted and his hopes had gone after an eight at the eleventh. Duncan started brightly but after taking seven at both the tenth and eleventh he ran up a five at the twelfth where he three-putted. By his own admission he gave up at this point, after which he played the last six holes in one under fours. His putting was described as pathetic. 'In cricket language, it was of the googly type. Whenever he struck the ball it leaped into the air as if he were lofting a stymie.' The veteran J.H. Taylor, 'who, after the first day's debacle had looked like Napoleon on Elba, fought with teeth patriotically set for his 78' to finish on 153.

In 1926 Mussolini cast a different shadow to the one he was to create by the time of the Second World War and understanding the intent of Anthony Spalding writing for the *New York Times* is not easy. In the report of the second day his article included a paragraph headed 'Hagen is a Mussolini' which stated:

When play started again, Walter Hagen, who led the field with a 68, was a sort of Mussolini who would dictate by his play the fate of the majority of his rivals. He reveled in his position, nor did he jeopardize it by being late. He was on view a half hour before his name was called. Hagen's golf, however, was not of the dictator type. He took 77 for 145. The links Mussolini was deposed by Jones and Melhorn, but Hagen, Freddie McLeod, Al Watrous, George Von Elm, Cyril Walker, Tommy Armour and Emmett French fill leading positions in the Mussolini ministry.

At the end of the second day the first eight named in Spalding's report, all Americans, filled the first eight places on the leader board.

At the close of play on the second day the leader board was:

W. Melhorn (USA)	70	74	144
Mr R.T. Jones Jnr (USA)	72	72	144
Walter Hagen (USA)	68	77	145
Al Watrous (USA)	71	75	146
F. McLeod (USA)	71	75	146
Mr. Geo Von Elm (USA)	75	72	147
Cyril Walker (USA)	79	71	150
Tom. Armour (USA)	74	76	150
A. Compston (unattached)	76	74	150
T. Barbour (Cavendish, Buxton)	77	73	150

CHAPTER THIRTEEN

The final day

In 1926, as in the years before and after, the championship players played 36 holes on the final day, the Friday. This was to allow them to be back behind the counter in the professional's shop at their home club on the Saturday, so that they might tend to the needs of the members. How things have changed. Now a player crawls around the course, playing eighteen holes in five hours or so on the Saturday and then does the same again on the Sunday. A preserved copy of the starting sheet for the final day in 1926 shows that Jones and Watrous teed off for their first round at 9.18am and for their second round at 1.18pm. In between the two rounds they had time to go back to Jones's hotel for lunch and a rest!

Coverage in the national papers of the two rounds played inevitably tends to concentrate more on the fourth round than the third, but the latter still provided much of interest. The weather was kind, with another day of brilliant sunshine and a north-westerly wind that dried the course even more. The greens were running ever faster and the players had a struggle to coax the ball near to each hole. Among the early starters was the redoubtable J.H. Taylor, now aged 56, who was winning championships before Jones was born. His first Open win had been some 32 years earlier, in 1894. He had announced that this was to be the last Open in which he would compete.

Darwin perceived him 'saying to himself that at least England should die game, and he did go to his death with a magnificent gesture. More perfectly accurate play could hardly be imagined. He holed one or two good putts on the way out, but on the whole he was certainly not lucky with his putts. All the way home the ball was shivering on the brink, and heaven knows what he might have achieved had it dropped. Out in 33, he continued to play the most perfect golf all the way home against the breeze, and was left with a four for a 70. Then, at last, the strain of the great effort told. He hooked his iron shot into a bunker and although he chipped out beautifully, he could not quite get his four.' The *Scotsman* noted how 'It was great to see Taylor's second shots coming up to those fast greens, hitting the target of turf among the bunkers and pulling up.'

The other British players continued to fall away. Barber's third round was a 78. Havers disappointed those clinging to hope by going out in 40 and coming back in 42. The 71 by H.A. Gaudin and 72 by Abe Mitchell were really a matter of too little, too late. Compston's third round started out dramatically, playing the first five holes in 2, 4, 4, 4, 3 but by the time he reached the twelfth much of the momentum was lost. At the sixth he hit his approach over the green. In the holes that ensued he was in bunker, sandhill and rough, having a six at the seventh, a five at the eighth and another six at the eleventh.

The golf correspondent of the *Glasgow Herald* described what happened next:

> I was wandering out with Mehlhorn, and went over from the sixth to the twelfth to see how Compston was getting on, and there he was, standing on top of a sandhill, a wild-looking figure, bareheaded, his hair flying in the wind, and obviously in distress. He had pushed his drive into a bunker, and was faced with the nerve-shattering ordeal of pitching out and over the hill on to a narrow strip of green, with a plantation just behind. He got too well out, and his ball went flying into the wood. Someone shouted that he was out of bounds. Then someone said he was not.

His marker, a lady, advised him that this area was, under a local rule, out of bounds and suggested he might wish to go back and play another ball. Compston preferred the advice of an unofficial bystander and elected to play from within the plantation, saying, 'Well I am going to play it from here.' Resuming the *Glasgow Herald* account, 'the ball lay in a horrid position in sand, and with a narrow avenue between two sets of trees as the only way to the green. It was a difficult shot. He ran it on to the green with a straight-faced club, and very nearly got a 4.' But the question of out-of-bounds still had to be addressed.

The *New York Times* described how Compston, 'being obstinate, thought he knew better, and so sinned against the light, played out of the plantation and thus committed suicide.' The local rule clearly identified the area as being out of bounds and Compston was subsequently disqualified by Norman Boase, chairman of the R&A's Championship Committee. With Compston went the last slim chance of a British player contending.

Melhorn had a torrid third round. Having put himself in an overnight position from which he might seize the great prize, his fall was sad to witness. He found far too many bunkers (three in the first five holes) and twice missed putts from within two feet of the hole. He had a brief moment of elation at the 543-yard seventh when his second shot, a full brassie, hit the flag and ended just a few inches from the hole. However, at the eighth he sliced two drives onto the railway line, for which the penalty in those days was just a single shot, and took two shots in a bunker at the ninth. Out in 40 left him too much to do and he came back in 39, missing a short putt to finish in 79. This meant that from leading overnight he went to lunch eight shots behind the leader.

Of the other Americans, Fred McLeod fell away with a 76 which included 36 putts. Around the turn he was bunkered on three consecutive holes and he missed three short putts on the way home. Joe Kirkwood went out in a promising 35 but took 43 on the back nine. George Von Elm played better than he scored and what should have been a 72 became a 76.

The star of the morning was Al Watrous, who by coincidence was playing with Jones in both morning and afternoon on the final day. Playing together meant Jones and Watrous could watch each other's play and the day soon had the feel of a match between the two as first one then the other gained an advantage. Jones started the day two ahead of Watrous and when the latter was short with his shot at the first to take four strokes, Jones was three ahead. Jones gave one of these shots back at the third where he had a five.

Both were bunkered at the fourth but had contrasting results from playing out. Watrous chipped out of the bunker to within six inches of the hole and got his four. Jones came out too cleanly with his niblick and his ball carried far over the green and the heads of the spectators into long grass. He came out weakly and 'throwing his club petulantly at his caddie, he took his putter and registered his first 6 of the week.' They were now level again.

While Watrous was steady on the way out, Jones found four bunkers on the front nine. At the seventh he took an iron shot for safety with his second and, as is so often the case, the safety shot found a bunker from where he played a superb recovery and got his birdie four, which Watrous matched. Jones continued to struggle at the ninth, playing a weak bunker shot for a four, while Watrous holed a four-yard putt for a two that gave him a two-shot margin over Jones in what was by now a head-to-head.

On the back nine the two players continued to give the large crowd an exhibition of fine shot-making. Jones had nine consecutive pars, recovering from being bunkered at the fourteenth with a single putt. Watrous had the agony of a missed short putt at the twelfth for what would have been a birdie and also dropped a stroke at the short fifteenth. He did however hole a ten-yard putt for a birdie three at the fourteenth and a four-yard putt at the eighteenth for a 69, the only sub-70 round of the day. He was now two shots ahead of Jones, who had gone round in 73. The rest of the field did not seem to exist.

There was however still the ever-present menace of Hagen, who went out an hour and a half after Jones and Watrous. His game was still patchy and in his morning round he found seven bunkers, though from four of those he did get up and down in two shots. He played the first six holes in two under fours but a cut drive at the seventh, carrying over the green at the eighth and finding a bunker at the ninth meant he was out in 36. At the tenth he hooked his tee shot into sandhills, played two shots in the bunker and holed a 30-foot putt for a five. Off the tee at the twelfth he was in rough but got his par with a pitch and putt. He missed from five feet at the thirteenth and at the following three holes was either bunkered or in tiger country. He came back in 39, finishing with a birdie three at the last hole to be four behind Watrous and two behind Jones. His menace, however, was not extinguished.

It is not known how long Jones and Watrous took for their third round, but with four hours between the tee-off times of the third and fourth rounds they still had plenty of time to kill. Jones looked after the inexperienced Watrous with such consideration that it could be postulated that he would have derived great joy from seeing Watrous win. In 1927 he recalled, 'Hagen was starting late that morning, and I told Al we'd better get away from the course and relax a bit; it's about the worst thing you can do, standing around the board waiting for some close rival to come in.'

Jones had a room at the large Majestic Hotel, some half a mile from the course. Jones described how 'we went to the hotel and took off our shoes and lay down and had a bit of luncheon. It was a killing thing on both of us, being the leaders and playing together. But it's the break of the game. And I remember telling Al, as we started back to the club for the last round, to remember that the champion and runner-up were in our pair. He's a great boy, Al Watrous.'

Keeler's account throws more light on the interlude:

I always liked the way Bobby advised his young professional rival to leave the scoreboard and go back with him to the hotel between rounds. The boys went up to our room, and I pulled their shoes off and they lay down on the twin beds while I ordered their frugal luncheon. I pulled down the shades, and I heard Bobby tell Al for goodness sake not to take a nap. That is almost certainly fatal, between rounds. It is not only heroes of fiction who can be courtly and sportsmanlike. Golf has supplied its counterparts of Saladin and Coeur de Lion.

For two golfers who were spending the day at each other's throats on the course, the way Jones looked after Watrous has to be seen as most generous. It was a gesture that stayed with Watrous throughout his life. His son Tom recalled, 'Whenever Dad spoke of Jones, it was never just his ability, but what a gentleman he was. I'm convinced that influenced Dad. He (Dad) was not an educated man, but he had an aura about him – always extremely gentlemanly. I picked up on that when I was a very small boy. I think he owed that to Bobby Jones.'

Lunch and rest over, they headed back to the course. On arrival at the players' entrance, Jones realised he had left his competitor's badge back at the hotel. Showing the merits of officialdom at its best, the man on the gate failed to recognise the most famous golfer in the world and refused him admission. Without any fuss, Jones moved over to the public gate and paid his two shillings and sixpence so that he might be allowed in. As this was the first year of admission charges it can be stated with confidence that this was the first time any player, let alone a subsequent champion, had to pay to get into the course and play his last round.

By this stage the fourth round was under way. Abe Mitchell improved on his 72 in the morning with a 71 in the afternoon, the best 36 score of the day, which lifted him to eventual fifth place. He was joined on 299 by Tom Barber of Cavendish, who recovered from his third-round 78 with a closing 71. Fred McLeod fell away with a 79 for 301. The rest of the field were out of reckoning. Melhorn's grim day continued as he followed his morning 79 with an afternoon 80, his last two rounds totalling fifteen more shots than his first two. Tommy Armour's putting had left him by this stage and he closed with an 80.

Of the golfers of earlier years, James Braid of Walton Heath had 82-75-73-79 for 311, Alex Herd of Moor Park 81-76-75-76 for 308 and Edward 'Ted' Ray of Oxhey 78-80-74-80 for 312. After his morning heroics, J.H. Taylor of Mid-Surrey could not maintain his momentum and had an 80 for 304. His performance was nevertheless remarkable. Now aged 55, it was some 32 years since his first Open Championship win in 1894 and thirteen years since his last in 1913. The American amateur and Walker Cup player George Von Elm had an error-free last round of 72 for 295 and what turned out to be a share of third place, but never threatened the leaders.

As far as the main drama was concerned there were only three players to watch in the last round. First out at 1.18pm were Jones and Watrous locked in close combat – Watrous on 215 and Jones two strokes behind. Two shots further back was the ever-dangerous Hagen, who teed off at 2.48pm.

The duel was there for all to see. Worrying about Hagen would have to be put off till later. The vast crowd knew that Jones and Watrous was the pair to go with and the consequence was that Jones in particular was swallowed up by the throng dashing forward after each shot to claim the best vantage point from which to watch the next shot. The surge of support was for Jones who was described as 'a quiet young man dressed in brown knickers and jersey, and a cap which he pulled far over his eyes to keep away the fierce glare of the sun.'

The mental and physical strain took its toll in a way that was visible to all. Darwin wrote, 'One felt sorry for the two men, who towards the end were clearly so done that a good hard push would have sent either reeling.' The *Scotsman* talked of 'Thirty-six holes of deadly combat in which every stroke was vital. Every nerve was strained, and every move on the fateful board could be seen by both, an ordeal of the links more dramatic, more wracking, and testing for two young players, to whom this golden opportunity meant fame for all time and beyond imagination.'

It was not a happy arrangement for either of the players; certainly not for Watrous, less experienced in playing to such a gallery. Early in the last round he wobbled a little, dropping a shot to Jones at the third. At the fifth he had a serious disaster, taking a five, but Jones took three putts and though he squared the match, he missed the chance to edge ahead.

At the long seventh Watrous played 'a really grand cleek shot' to the green and Jones, who was bunkered to the right of the green, was again one behind. Worse was to follow at the short ninth, once again the jinx hole for Jones. Watrous was through the green while Jones put his tee shot safely on. Watrous, apparently nerveless, ran his pitch close to get his three and Jones, perhaps a little unsettled, ran his first putt four feet past and missed the return. Turning for home, Watrous had regained his precious two-shot lead.

To the spectator, Jones appeared unflustered by the drama happening before his eyes, but inwardly the experience was searing him at every twist. As Greenwood saw it, 'Jones weathered it better and though he seemed the coolest person amongst the thousands whom the duel thrilled and excited to an extraordinary degree, despite the fact that Britain had no stake in it, he never relaxed for a moment in his historic quest.' Jones was to admit afterwards that he 'felt the personal duel aspect of the partnership. We were simply cutting each other's throats. I was desperately near to cracking.'

Jones had two big problems, to neither of which could he produce a solution. Firstly, his putting was completely off and for the eighteen holes he was to take 39 putts, three-putting on three occasions. Thankfully the rest of his game held up. Keeler described how 'He was playing golf in his best vein at the last – up to the green. And there the putts would simply not fall. In the sweeping wind he put his back into the big shots, hitting the ball farther and farther; he planted his approaches closer and closer to the flag – and missed the putts.'

Secondly, he could see no signs of the tension getting to Watrous. Why was his game not beginning to crack? When was all the pressure going to make this innocent young man show signs of frailty? Both had taken 36 for the first nine and Jones knew that he was destined to finish second unless Watrous began to be vulnerable.

The first indication that Watrous was, after all, being affected by all that was going on around him came at the very next hole. He pulled his tee shot behind a large sandhill and Jones had one of the two shots back. He had a chance of squaring – and it is right to use match play terms by this stage – at the very next hole where Watrous was in the rough but again Jones took three putts. At the long thirteenth Watrous had a splendid four and with five holes to go was two shots to the good.

Two shots behind with five holes to play, with a putter that was stone cold, Jones knew there was nothing he could do unless an opening came. What happened next to Watrous was dramatic. As Darwin noted, 'then quite unexpectedly, almost in the hour of victory, he broke. He overran the fourteenth hole with his approach putt, and missed coming back. He missed a really short one at the fifteenth, pushing the ball out in a way that always betrays nerves.' He had run the first putt four feet past and his return putt missed the hole by some way.

The *Scotsman* observed that 'It was at the fourteenth that Watrous … gave way under the tension. His short game suddenly went weak there. That mysterious something crept into his strokes just at the pinch, and he was short [*sic*] and took three putts.' Leaving the fifteenth green, the players were now level and Watrous was relieved to settle down at the sixteenth and get a steady four.

Still there was drama mixed with an element of comedy to come. At the sixteenth both drove well and Darwin describes what happened next:

On the sixteenth came an incident of which a friend has recently reminded me; it gives force to the ruthless doctrine that someone ought to murder a photographer *pour encourager les autres*. Watrous had played his second to the green and Bobby had got half-way up with some pitching club when a fiend with a camera stepped out and tried to snap him. Bobby stopped and began again, and again the photographer tried. This time he was metaphorically lynched; he was shooed out of the way, and Bobby, by a considerable display of control, pitched safely onto the green and the hole was halved in fours.

In match play terms, all square and two to go as they headed for the seventeenth tee.

CHAPTER FOURTEEN

A teaspoonful of sand

'A teaspoonful too much sand might have meant
irretrievable ruin.'

BERNARD DARWIN

As he left the seventeenth tee, Jones must have felt his stomach in a total knot. By now the British Open was no longer medal play but raw match play – his biggest threat was walking alongside him. So when it was all square in match play terms with two holes to play, what had he done? Tightening up, his right hand had crawled over his left at impact and the result was a high hanging draw, with the ball disappearing from his view.

But he knew where the ball had finished: in just about the worst place possible on the hole – scrubby wasteland with who knew what sort of lie? To make things worse, Watrous had done just what Jones would have done in similar circumstances: choked down slightly and hit a drive of decent length safely down the right half of the fairway.

By now each player was in his cocoon of concentration. Jones was trying to focus on his own plight, but was still aware that Watrous was set to regain his lead. All Watrous had to do was to put his next shot onto the green. It was too much to hope that tension would get to him at this stage. Before he played his shot, he came across to see the plight of Jones's ball. What he saw gave him considerable comfort, as there was little prospect that Jones could make any great progress from where he was. Watrous made a swing that looked just as smooth as those of the rest of the round, but perhaps some tension did have its influence as his shot pulled up short and only just made the front of the putting surface.

When those watching saw where Jones's ball lay, they could see that the shot played by Watrous was likely to suffice. As part of the preparation for the Open, large areas of earth had been stripped of their grass covering and left open to the elements as expanses of sand broken up with shrubs and tufts. There lay the ball of the Georgian amateur, on sand with all of 175 yards to go to the green.

The almost impossible challenge presented can be seen from figure 1, taken from a detailed survey of the course made in 1934. The hole is a dramatic dogleg from right to left. From the right half of the fairway the green is visible and accessible. From the left-hand side the green is completely obscured from view, but that is less of a problem than the intervening hazards. Playing directly for the green called for a shot of nothing other than perfection. Anything short would call for another nightmare recovery shot.

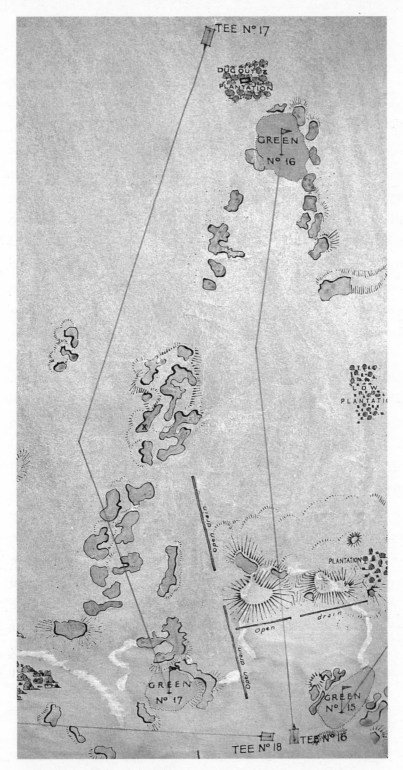

Figure 1. The 1934 survey of the seventeenth hole. X marks the spot from
which the shot was played. The intimidating challenge is obvious.

The sensible shot was to play out sideways or a few yards forwards and then hope against hope that an outstanding third shot might yet save the day. Jones considered this option but not for too long. He had come all this way to win, not to finish second. The old Jones, rendered volatile by the destructive effect of his temperament, would have gone for the impossible shot but failed. The new Jones, in which temperament had metamorphosed into strain, dealt with the crisis differently. Instead of weakening, he became stronger: but in place of outward fury, the price was internal erosion. The bigger the challenge, the more his game rose to meet it. A few years earlier he had revealed his ability to play supreme shots under pressure on the last hole of his 1923 US Open play-off against Bobby Cruickshank, but this shot was dramatically more of a challenge, not only of technique and temperament, but also of inner steel.

His own account, written in 1927, is matter of fact. He writes:

The seventeenth at St. Anne's is a hole of 411 yards, with apparently acres of sand along the left side of the fairway, all done out in dunes. The hole bends to the left and the sand is not a good place to play your second from. Added to the native disadvantage of a sand lie, from the position in which I found my ball after a slightly pulled drive I could not see the green at all. Al Watrous, with whom I was paired, had lost a lead of two strokes and we were level with two holes to play. Here he had a good drive and his second was on the green. As suggested, it was a critical position.

The only way I could get a good look at the green, and what lay between it and my ball, was to walk far out to the right, nearly across the fairway. I did this. The prospect was not precisely encouraging. I had to hit a shot with a carry of close to 175 yards, and hit it on a good line, and stop the ball very promptly when it reached the green – if it reached the green. This, off dry sand, though the ball luckily lay clean, was a stiff assignment. You know, an eighth of an inch too deep, and the shot expires right in front of your eyes. And if your blade is a thought too high – I will dismiss this harrowing reflection.

Anyway, I played the shot and it came off, and the ball stopped closer to the pin than Al's, and he took three putts.

'Anyway, I played the shot and it came off' must be the ultimate example of understatement.

This singular shot was significant from a variety of angles. From the host club's point of view, it meant that the 1926 British Open was instantly more memorable than those that preceded it or followed it for several years. From Jones's point of view, it probably saved his sanity and also secured his reputation on the world stage as a golfer of the highest order. For those assessing Jones's place in golfing history, it became a focal point in revealing his mettle and defining his nature.

Such is the importance of this single shot that it is worth examining in detail how it was reported at the time and since. Bernard Darwin wrote about it in *The Times*, George

Greenwood in *Golf Illustrated* and the *Daily Telegraph*, and Al
Laney in *Following the Leaders*. While many claimed over the
following years to have seen the stroke, the truth is somewhat
different. In the Royal Lytham & St Anne's yearbook of 1998,
an article appeared recording the clear recollection of a
former captain of the club, Ian Hargreave, who was almost
certainly the last person living who had seen the famous shot.
At that time he was aged 85, having been a young man in his
early teens in 1926.

One interesting aspect of his memories is that while there
were huge numbers of spectators around the green, the
number back down the fairway wasn't that many. In several
texts it is stated that after Jones's shot, someone was heard to
say, 'There goes $100,000.' Instead, what was said was by the
American Walker Cup player William Fownes *before* Watrous
played his second shot. 'At the moment when Watrous was
about to play his second,' reminisced Bernard Darwin in *Golf
Between Two Wars*, 'Mr. Fownes was justified in saying to me as
he did: "He's got this shot for 100,000 dollars."'

What is beyond doubt is that the shot played by Jones
was extraordinary. Even nearly twenty years later, Darwin still
viewed it with rapt admiration. In the same book, published
in 1944, he wrote:

> Bobby's ball lay in a shallow bunker and it lay clean, but
> he was 170 yards or more from the flag and between him
> and it were the sandhills. He took what I think he called
> his mashie-iron (it now reposes a sacred relic in the St
> Anne's club) and hit the ball perfectly clean, playing it
> somewhat out into the wind so that it came to finish on the

green and nearer the hole than his opponent. Admittedly the ball lay clean as clean could be and this was the kind of shot that he might very well have played in a practice game, but in the circumstances, when a teaspoonful too much sand might have meant irretrievable ruin, it was a staggering shot, and it staggered poor Al Watrous. He took three putts, Bobby got down in two and everybody felt that that shot had settled it.

The contemporary report in the *Daily Telegraph* described it thus:

> When Mr. Jones, at the dog-legged seventeenth, put his drive into the long stretch of sand and bents away on the left the position indeed looked black. But, after much study, Mr. Jones played one of the finest shots ever witnessed in a championship, and one that will live in history. Taking a No. 4 iron, he thumped the ball slap on to the middle of the green nearly 180 yards away. This was so unexpected a development that Watrous, who had visions of getting in front again, took three putts and was one stroke to the bad.

The account in the *Scotsman* of Jones's last five holes reads:

> Mr. Jones came along that stretch in 43444, terribly relentless blows in the crisis. His golf contained one heroic stroke produced in time of stress with the mastery we now know. He pulled his drive to the seventeenth

into sand and star grass, and from this he hit a beautiful recovery, a stroke of about 150 yards, which carried over the shoulder of the hillock and finished in the middle of the green. The crowd broke into a roar of applause at this effort. They knew it for what it was, a victory stroke, and they followed the drama to the close.

In *The Times*, Darwin reported that

> He [Watrous] rallied well, but was finally knocked out by a tremendous thrust of his enemy's at the 17th. Watrous was right down the middle, and Mr. Jones away in a waste of sand on the left. Watrous played the odd, and reached the green, and then Mr. Jones played the most superb full iron shot. True, he was lucky enough to have a clean-lying ball on the sand, but, even so, what a shot at such a point, and it killed Watrous, who was short and took three putts.

George Greenwood's account in *Golf Illustrated* states that after the sixteenth:

> The excitement now grew fast and furious. Something had to give and it did at the seventeenth, a dog-legged hole swinging from right to left. Running down the left hand side of the course is a wilderness of sand and broken country with huge tufts of sea grass sticking out here and there. When Bobby hooked his drive into the wilderness, and Watrous hit one straight down the middle we thought the end had surely come. What

seemed more likely than that Watrous would nip in and clinch the matter once and for all.

Jones waded into the sand with his favourite mashie-iron and, lo and behold! a miracle happened. A cloud of sand spurted into the air, and a few seconds later the frenzied spectators were astounded to see the ball drop slap on to the middle of the green, give a couple of feeble hops and stop. This shot will live in history not only because it won a championship, but because of the manner in which it was executed. Considering the heavy lie, and the fact that the shot was all carry over 175 yards of terrible country it was a marvellous shot. It was a shot that so astounded Watrous that once more he took three putts. He was now one shot to the bad, having lost three shots in the last four holes.

The description in the *Glasgow Herald* reads:

Watrous from the tee was in the middle of the fairway. Jones walked from his ball to the fairway and carefully surveyed the ground. Watrous, who had to play the odd, went over and had a look at Jones's lie to weigh probabilities. Watrous just got to the edge of the green. Jones had to get to the green or in all probability lose the championship, which now seemed, barring Hagen, to be within his grasp. He took a No. 4 iron and with the courage of a lion hit a magnificent shot onto the middle of the green. Watrous, shaken by this shattering blow, took three from the edge of the green, and now for the first time in the round, Jones was in the lead for the four round aggregate.

The aforementioned account of the 1963 club captain
Ian Hargreave, recollected in the club's 1998 yearbook, reads
as follows:

> I have seen all the Open championships played over our
> course. The first in 1926 was won by Bobby Jones. I saw
> the famous shot on the 17th hole – a remarkable stroke.
> In view of the conflicting and confusing accounts written
> since, it is worth defining just what Jones did. The area
> to the left of the seventeenth where the ball lay wasn't
> a bunker as such – there was a forty yard stretch of bare
> sand with occasional shrubs and tufts of grass, just like
> there still is at Pine Valley. Jones's ball lay on sand in this
> wild expanse and to play the shot he did called for great
> courage and ability.
>
> The club he used for that wonderful shot was
> later presented to Royal Lytham. It was a mashie, the
> equivalent of the five iron of today and it was hung
> inside the clubhouse. Tommy Catlow and I got into
> severe trouble with Pattirson the porter for taking it
> out on the short course for a few practice shots. It was
> subsequently fastened down!

The last eyewitness account, perhaps the most revealing,
rests with American journalist Al Laney:

> Since Hagen was so far behind Jones and Watrous, I went
> with the other two. Jones gave me the fits. He was not
> playing the sort of golf that was needed to close the gap,
> but he did finally get even at the 16th after struggling

for many of his pars. Then he promptly pulled his tee shot at the 17th into serious trouble to set the stage for the climax. The 17th measured a few more yards than 400, and the hole bent a little to the left around a large, rolling sweep of sand. Jones's ball lay clean on the sand, but between it and the green were a nearby bunker and a series of dunes. He was a long way from the green, probably 180 yards, and could not see the flag. Neither could I from where I stood, and I did not want to move. I wanted to see the shot itself, and I was almost afraid to look.

Watrous had hit a good straight drive, and, playing first, he put his ball on the green. Jones walked straight across the fairway from left to right and stood there looking first at the green, then at the spot where he had put his tee shot. I wondered what he was thinking, looking first one way then back, and I have wondered a thousand times since what it is that tournament players think about when they stand there, putting off the moment for taking action. Not that Jones dawdled. Far from it. He always decided quickly, then went to work.

Now he looked, came back with his mind already made up, and what I remember more acutely than the shot itself was how drawn and almost ill Bob's face appeared as he stepped into the sand and settled his feet. Then he struck the ball with a mashie-iron, about a no. 4 by later gradings. A big shout down the fairway told us that the ball had safely reached the green. When Watrous eventually took three putts, Jones moved a stroke ahead.

What made it one of the finest shots ever brought off in championship play? The ball lay on dry sand. A fraction too much sand, and the ball might hardly move at all and end up in a worse place. A fraction too little sand or none at all, and the ball might skitter and run into some really horrid spot. With the target out of sight, the stroke also had to be judged exactly so that the ball would become airborne instantly, carry 175 yards or more, and stop quickly after reaching the green. It was only after I heard the shot discussed that I came to have some understanding of its difficulty and the boldness, technical mastery and even artistry involved in bringing it off.

One person who missed seeing this extraordinary shot was O.B. Keeler who witnessed everything else Jones did. He later confessed, 'I did NOT see that shot. I followed that last round through the thirteenth hole where Bobby was still two behind Watrous then I switched over to the clubhouse hoping against hope that if I quit watching the luck would change … It did. It did. I was over at the clubhouse in the bar taking on a liberal belt of antifreeze when the news came in.'

In retrospect, it is clear that this was to Jones the defining shot of his golfing career. The inward forces driving Jones on to success and giving him the ability to produce such a shot in such a pressure-laden situation extracted a high price for this gift, as is revealed in the telling observations of Laney, giving an insight into how playing to this level of performance was at the same time consuming Jones from within. Now pale and almost sucked dry by the drama, Jones walked with the shaken Watrous to the eighteenth tee.

CHAPTER FIFTEEN

The final hole

By the time he was ready to drive from the eighteenth tee, Watrous was physically and mentally spent. His long game had held up under pressure he had never experienced before, but his putter had fatally let him down at the fourteenth and fifteenth holes to allow Jones to draw level. When he had reached the safety of the seventeenth green, knowing where his opponent's ball lay in the sand after his drive, he must have sensed that the moment was his. With disbelief he had seen Jones's ball appear on the green. The shot had 'seemed to slay poor Watrous.' By now the putter must have felt like a serpent in his hands and his third three-putt in four holes meant he stood on the last tee one shot behind the lead.

Without any hesitation, Jones had hit a long, straight drive down the last hole, though it skirted rather close to a bunker. Despite his best efforts, Watrous pulled his tee shot into the very bunker Jones had just narrowly avoided. From there the young man from Chicago hit a brave second shot which ran onto the green but then disappeared into a bunker on the left side of the putting surface. The account in the *Scotsman* gives an indication of the state of Jones as he came to his ball:

> The hero of the moment looked worn out. His features were drawn under their bronze, though he walked up the last fairway with a cigarette between his lips, but one can imagine his feelings in the strain under which he played to victory.

He played his second safely onto the green five yards from the hole. The huge crowd of some 6,000 was eventually marshalled into a big oblong and then fell into a great hush. Watrous came out of the bunker and holed out in five.

There were still distractions to be addressed and before his first putt, Jones had to step away from his ball and ask the photographers formed into a platoon on the balcony to desist from moving. He then rolled his first putt close and when he tapped in for a four, the crowd cheered to the echo. He had a two-shot margin over his courageous friend. However, as long as Hagen was still out there, the result remained in doubt.

Describing how Jones and Watrous finished, the *Daily Telegraph* commented:

> As the fates ordained, he was engaged in a titanic fight with one man only, and that man happened to be his partner, Watrous. Both men were on the verge of collapse; in fact one man did collapse, and that was Watrous. Mr. Jones kept his head and his nerve to the end.

Jones had played the treacherous last five holes in level par for a 74, his worst round of the four, and poor Watrous had returned a 78.

Everyone saw it as a match rather than a stroke play event and Darwin said, 'It had been a great match, and however much one rejoiced over Mr. Jones, one could not but be sorry for Watrous. He had made a great fight of it in circumstances as strenuous and exhausting as can be imagined. The excitement was intense, the crowd very big, and, though everybody admired Watrous, every man, woman, and child on the ground was, in the language, "looking for Bobby."'

The two left the green arm in arm, Watrous to brood on the opportunity missed and Jones to slump into a chair in the corner of the smoking room. Although both sensed that the climax had established the winner, there was of course one unresolved matter. As Darwin put it, 'Still it was too early to make merry over Mr. Jones's victory, for was not the terrible Hagen coming?' Given the time the players took to complete a round in those days, Hagen would not have completed his first nine before Jones had finished.

Not only was it going to be ages before Hagen reappeared but the rudimentary communications of the age created an element of chaos. Before he vanished in the direction of the far end of the course it was known that he had started strongly, playing the first five holes in 3, 4, 4, 4, 3. Then the rumours started coming in. The first was that he had reached the turn in 34, which was cause enough for concern. Then it was said that he was 33 out, then an intimidating 32, which would give him a real tilt at the score Jones had posted.

At this point Keeler's agitation overcame him and he left Jones upstairs as he made his way to the Press tent. On the way he came across a man who told him that Hagen was two under fours after thirteen. This was indeed ominous as it could herald a 71, which would be enough for Hagen to win. With a rising sense of despair, Keeler reached the Press tent, where a British reporter 'was wrangling over the telephone much as we do in America, but with a different accent. Finally he said Hagen was two over 4's at the fourteenth. I turned right around and went back to the smoking room and shook hands with Bobby Jones.'

It transpired that Hagen had dropped shots at the seventh and eighth where he three-putted. Then at the ninth, which according to Darwin 'had slain 10,000 during this championship' he was bunkered and dropped another shot. He had gone out in 36, so for a 71 he would need to come back in 35, which presented a challenge. In the entire week, Jones was the only player who had been able to do so. Hagen's putt for a birdie at the twelfth lipped the hole. At the thirteenth he took three putts, missing from two feet, and after a bunkered tee shot at the short fifteenth dropped another shot there. After the sixteenth he needed to play the last two holes in six strokes to tie with Jones – an unlikely but not impossible outcome. He had a crowd of 'between two and three thousand' milling around to see if the miracle could be worked.

At the seventeenth it looked as if it might. He came within a hair's breadth of a three, the ball stopping on the lip of the hole. A two at the last? Hagen was perhaps the only person who saw it as an option – why shouldn't he manage to hole his second? What transpired next was unclear in the matter of details at the time and has become increasingly more unclear since. Two facts are beyond dispute. Firstly, his second shot ended up in a bunker at the back of the green. Secondly, he took two shots to emerge from the bunker and holed out in six to complete his round in 76 and tie for third place with George Von Elm on 295. This was his worst finishing place since 1921.

After a good drive he had faced a second shot of 120 yards. According to the *Daily Telegraph*:

> He now required a 2 on the last hole. I do not know whether Hagen tried to hole his second shot, a long mashie; but the fact is that the ball ran past the flag and plunged into a bunker at the back of the green. He failed to get out, and instead of a 2 there came a 6. If he had been content with a 4 he would have been second; but this was not good enough for Hagen, who was out to catch Mr. Jones. A very gallant effort failed.

The bunker was in place of what was formerly a flowerbed.

The American view is given in the *New York Times*, which reported:

> Hagen was out at the far end of the course with his teeth clenched in his most hostile and menacing manner. It may sound unsportsmanlike, but the crowd was pulling for his defeat. Hagen had to do 71 to win and 72 to tie. Everybody hoped and believed he could not do it, and when he was left with a pitch to tie and the ball

raced across the green from the clubhouse garden [*sic*] everybody heaved a sigh and felt relieved.

Other accounts have him walking all the way up to the hole to inspect it before walking all the way back to his ball. Some have him sending his caddie forward to attend the flag and the ball nearly pitching in.

The most detailed account is found in *The Walter Hagen Story* which Hagen wrote many years later and which was published in 1956. There is a suggestion from more than one episode in this book that by that stage of his life, repeated telling of tales and happenings had resulted in a blurring in his own recollection of the distinction between fact and legend. Hagen's entire life had been one built on the aura and mystique of his existence and bravado was a stock part of his life:

> I was playing in the British Open at Royal Lytham and St Anne's and I was trying to catch Bobby Jones at the last and deciding hole. Bobby had finished with a total of 291 and was watching from the balcony of the clubhouse. My drive from the eighteenth tee was as good as I could hope for, but it still left me with an approach shot of 150 yards to the green. I might hole out with a perfect shot and a lot of luck. It had been done. And to tie with Jones I would need an eagle 2.
>
> I walked some steps away from my ball to examine the lie of the land. Then I asked the official scorer if he would go down and hold the flag. I spoke quietly and he did not understand. I asked him again, and this time a

few people around me heard the request, which I had not intended. The official went on down the fairway, but he remained on a mound short of the green.

Now I had to walk half the distance and tell him again to take the flag. By yelling, 'I want you to hold the flag' I found myself informing the ten thousand in the gallery (as well as Bobby Jones and J.H. Taylor on the balcony) just what I intended to do. However, I then realised that by concentrating the attention of the gallery on the official, standing 150 yards from my ball, I had eased my own tension. With their eyes on him, not me, and with their thoughts concerned with 'the blooming ass down there holding the flag' I could concentrate completely on playing the shot. Should I miss he would be the goat for taking the flag at such a distance.

Now that I had everything set, I returned to my ball, carefully took my stance and played. The shot was better than I dared hope for. I saw the ball head straight for the pin, land just on the edge of the green, and roll towards the hole. It had a one chance in a thousand of finding the cup. But I had hit it a bit too hard. It jumped over the hole – it would have hit the flag – and dropped into the shallow scooped-out sand trap at the back of the green. The warming part of the episode was that I got almost as much applause as if my ball had holed.

Bobby told me later, 'I turned my back on you, Walter. Because a guy with that much confidence would be fool lucky enough to make it.' Actually I believe I set up that situation to give the gallery a thrill, but I got just as much a thrill myself, for I thought I *might* make it.

If charitably inclined, one might let Hagen's account stand without comment, but it does have to be pointed out that with no other players to watch, all the golf writers attending would have been watching Hagen play the last hole. If his shot had been anywhere near the hole, comment would surely have been made in one or other of the papers of the time.

Perhaps the final word on how Hagen played the last hole should rightly rest with Al Laney, one of the most perceptive golf writers of the time. He wrote that 'the whole tournament really came down to a couple of shots, one justly celebrated because it won the title, the other legendary although it did not come off.' His description, already given, of the shot played by Jones on the seventeenth in the last round gave more insight than any other account and he also tells the real story of Hagen's last hole. He notes:

> The other famous shot at Lytham, I think, might well have been forgotten by all of us if it had not been kept alive by much retelling and dramatic rewriting. I am not at all sure that it was not actually born in the retelling. It was struck by Hagen long after Jones had finished and been congratulated. Hagen had a chance to catch Bob certainly. And there were reports that he was doing extraordinary things late in the afternoon. He was some holes back. I believed these reports. You could never be sure about Hagen, however slim the chance. That's what everyone said. It was good to keep an eye on him, and a lot of us did. However, when we came up the 18th fairway with him after his fine drive, we all knew his chance was gone.

The story told afterward was that Hagen made a great production of walking up to the green to make sure the flag was attended and that the attender should be alert and ready to yank the stick out to let the ball fall into the cup. Hagen, it is related, made gestures and said words that clearly conveyed to the crowd that the great Sir Walter never played for second place. He was going for a first-place tie and a shot at victory in a play-off. And, the story goes, he played the shot only after making sure of the proper tension and suspense, and then came so close to holing it as to take your breath away.

This is a wonderful story and has become part of the game's fact and tradition. I am sorry to relate that I do not remember it that way, and this time I feel sure I am right. I stood in the gallery behind Hagen and what I remember is that the ball went all the way through the green, passing not really very close to the cup and winding up in a bunker.

I believe now that the whole thing was built on little that actually happened. Golfers often walked towards the green before making long approach shots, and thousands of approach shots that passed near the hole have ended up in bunkers. Hagen had long finished his competitive career and become one of the game's revered figures before I ever got around to bringing up this matter with him. I was on the point of speaking several times but something stopped me. I think I wanted it to be true.

When I did finally question him, he laughed and said something like the following: 'Don't you remember, son? I never deny any story about myself. I don't go around breaking down my image at this late stage in my life.' Walter was right, of course. One scuttles golf legends at one's peril.

What can be said for certain about Hagen's finish is that he took a six at the last to tie for third. Jones had exorcised his experiences in the 1921 Open and had won golf's oldest championship. Darwin wrote '"Bobby has won" was heard on all sides and so he had. It is difficult to understand why he does not win all championships.'

CHAPTER SIXTEEN

The presentation

Once Hagen's shot to the eighteenth passed the hole, there was no longer any doubt that the 24-year-old Georgian Mr Robert Tyre Jones Jnr had indeed won the British Open. He was the first American amateur to do so and only the third amateur since 1860, the other two being those great men of Hoylake, Mr John Ball Jnr and Mr Harold Hilton.

In the large upstairs smoking room of the clubhouse, now the Club Room, there were expressions of genuine joy and congratulations. It was said with justification that it was the most popular golfing victory ever seen in Britain. Jack Morris of Hoylake, the oldest of the professionals, was shaking Jones by the hand. Others more demonstrative were slapping him on the back or – in a singularly un-British manner – hugging him.

For his part Jones was just getting to the stage of being able to function. Towards the end of the round he commented that he had felt in a daze, to an extent dissociated from what was going on around him. Surrounding him and congratulating him were all the players whose best wishes he would thereafter treasure. From the previous decades were the three golfers who made up the Great Triumvirate, Harry Vardon, J.H. Taylor and James Braid, who between them had won sixteen British Open Championships. Also there was Ted Ray, pipe in hand, George Duncan, the Scot, and the distinguished amateur and former Open winner, Harold Hilton. Between them, the members of this galaxy were winners of some 40 championships.

Hilton was a member of St Anne's, as well as Hoylake and elsewhere, and his name featured around the honours board in the room, as he and John Ball had plundered many gold medals over the years, as well as winning the club's premier stroke play trophy, the Silver Iron, on several occasions. As everyone crowded around Jones, it was noteworthy how quiet he was.

Outside, the presentation table was put in place and to mark the nationality of the winner it was draped in a large stars and stripes. Few of the large crowd still present showed any inclination to disperse to head off home. They wanted to see Jones once more. Norman Boase, chairman of the Championship Committee, led him out. The club captain of that year, J.R. Dixon, had been in poor health to the extent that he had been unable to attend. A past captain, Colonel Topping, stood in for him. Topping had been the marker for Jones in an earlier round and Jones had confided in him, 'My golf is terrible.'

By this stage Hagen had laughed off his defeat and was in good spirits when he came up to the presentation table and gave Jones an oversized niblick. There is no record of what was said but Jones looked suitably perplexed as he received it. At last the Claret Jug was handed over and Jones was able to cradle it for what was to be the first of three wins in three consecutive appearances in the British Open Championship.

The *Glasgow Herald* reported on the speech by Jones at the presentation:

> At the presentation of the cup Jones made a gracious little speech of thanks. He had, he said, always wanted to have his name on this cup along with such names as Taylor, Vardon and Braid, even if it was at the bottom (Laughter). He did not know what they thought about it, but he always regarded Britain and America as one nation (Applause). He apologised to the crowd if he had been annoyed by them moving once or twice, but they must forgive him, for he had been so nervous all day he did not know what he had been doing (Laughter).

J.H. Taylor then spoke touchingly when he voiced the congratulations of all British golfers, and especially British professionals, to the man he was proud to claim as one of his greatest friends. He had tears running down his cheeks as he told the crowd that 'The greatest golfing prize has been won by the greatest golfer.'

Jones had great admiration for what Taylor had done in the third round. He wrote:

> To me, John Henry Taylor, 56-year-old English professional, was the hero of St. Anne's. John Henry shot a 71 in a hard wind in the third round, his gallant

effort to stave off the rush of the American invaders. It was better than I could do in any round. And when I am 56 years old! ... My hat is off, to John Henry.

Taylor also impressed Keeler, who said:

> In all the realm of sport, I never expect to see a more affecting sight than old John Henry Taylor, 56 years old, who had made a magnificent gesture for old England, with a 71 in the third round, making his little speech at the cup presentation; how he stood there, square and solid and bald of head, and with the tears running down his cheeks, congratulated the visitors and said Bobby was the greatest golfer who ever lived.

Darwin had no hesitation in stating his opinion 'that no greater, and no more accomplished, golfer has ever won a British championship. Certainly, and this is more to the point, no more modest, or generous golfer has ever won one.' He went on to say, 'I will hazard one other opinion, and it is the highest compliment I can pay to Mr. Jones's technical skill. I do not think, even though he won, that he was seen at his best, and I feel almost sure that in his own heart he was not satisfied with his game. He sets himself a terribly high standard, and he did not quite live up to it, but he played well enough to beat everybody else, and he is the best golfer in the world to-day.'

The modest way in which Jones accepted all the congratulations further enhanced his already considerable popularity. He revealed some of the problems that had affected his game. 'I did my best to win it,' he said, 'but my last round was the worst round of putting I have played in seven national championships, except once in the United States Open at Columbia. I lost confidence on the greens. I was dazed. I felt I was fighting a great personal duel with Watrous, and that we were cutting each other's throats.' He had taken ten more putts in the second round than he had in the first.

He recognised that it was only the frailty in the putting of Watrous that gave him his opportunity. 'More than once,' he added, 'I felt that I was desperately near to cracking. Relief only came through the failure of Watrous near the end of the struggle, when he took three putts on three greens.' He knew that his second shot to the seventeenth was crucial, pointing out that 'Probably the shot that won me the championship was the one from the great heaps of sand at the seventeenth hole. I took great care to find the line over the hills, and I was lucky to strike the green. Then I felt I was safe.'

It was clear that his amazing shot at the penultimate hole won the championship for the young American. The Scottish golf journalist Charlie Macfarlane had been spellbound when he had watched Jones play his perfect round at Sunningdale a couple of weeks earlier. A keen student of the game, he had previously played with distinction, including a spectacular win over the US amateur Chick Evans in the British Amateur in 1914. Now at St Anne's, Macfarlane came to Keeler after the presentation with tears streaming down his face.

Macfarlane asked, 'O.B., do you think Bobby would give me the club he made that shot with – the greatest shot in the history of British golf?' Keeler responded, 'I'm sure he will, Charlie. And I'll just go and get it for you now.' Keeler knew the club to be a favourite of Jones but when he put Macfarlane's plea to Bobby, there was no ready way of turning it down. Jones ruefully pointed out that it seemed to be a matter of losing championships or pet clubs. A few years later, Macfarlane presented the mashie to Royal Lytham & St Anne's Golf Club and it is still on display in the Club Room.

Hagen left the scene in characteristic mode. With him was his caddie who had accompanied him over from the States to carry not just his bag but, more importantly, the 30 clubs that Hagen took around the course. Hagen had, naturally, lived the high life at the Majestic Hotel in St Anne's, and hired a sumptuous Rolls-Royce to transport him around the district. The caddie was paid £10 per week, which was dramatically more than run-of-the-mill caddies earned. As the Rolls-Royce moved off down Clifton Drive, Hagen bounced golf balls off the road to be collected as souvenirs by the departing spectators.

A telegram of congratulations written in Latin arrived from Scotland. It took Jones and Keeler a little time to translate it, but they realised it was a model of modesty and good taste. Eventually they worked out that it said, 'Congratulations from a small nobody (*nemo parvo*) who was impudent enough to beat you.' It was from Andrew Jamieson who had triumphed over Jones in the British Amateur and who, by so doing, gave Jones the impetus to rearrange his sailings so he could, after all, play in the Open. Without that defeat, golfing history would have been different in so many ways. To Jones it was just one more element of the destiny that he sensed shaped his life.

In his interviews after winning, Jones was asked if he had made money from playing golf. Indicating that he had not, he said, 'I reckon this trip will leave me $1,500 out of pocket, but it has been worthwhile. There is no monetary value, as far as I'm concerned, in winning the British Open championship, but it is an honour which an American in particular is proud to hold.' In an editorial, the *Daily Telegraph* concluded that 'Mr. Jones, a quiet young man dressed in brown knickers and jersey, is a worthy champion in every respect. He is extremely modest, hates to talk about himself, and shuns the limelight as he would the plague.'

At the same time, Hagen in his interviews increased his own unpopularity in Britain. He pointed out that British players simply did not work hard enough at their game and used the word 'lazy'. He went on to say that it would be better for golf if the British could occasionally win their own Open, rather than let it become a showcase for the American supremacy. He seemed a little taken aback to find the *Observer* bristling and summarising his 'gratuitous little lecture' as 'ridiculous nonsense' and 'condescending frothiness'. An anonymous British player was quoted as saying that 'Hagen's reception stands decidedly frigid. His characteristics of largeness, newness, and expansiveness did not appeal to the blunt but very generous Northern heart.'

Some four weeks earlier, the caddie for Jones at Muirfield had been a young local Scot, Jack McIntire. After the dismay of the defeat by Jamieson, McIntire had also caddied for Jones at St Andrews in the Walker Cup. Keeler describes how the caddie responded to Jones's defeat in the Amateur: he 'would not admit that Bobby could be beaten, even after Andrew

Jamieson had sent him out of the British championship.'
Keeler observed:

> There is something to be said for Caledonian persistence,
> and Jack was a fair sample. 'I know he's the greatest of
> them all,' he said, tears streaming down his face after
> Bobby was beaten. 'You'll find me waiting at St. Anne's
> to show them all in the Open championship.'
> Simple faith and maybe a bit of Scottish Presbyterian
> predestination! Jack was waiting for Bobby at St. Anne's.
> He carried his clubs like a conquering hero through
> those four tremendous fighting rounds on a windswept
> course, when Bobby, never in front for a single round,
> turned up two strokes ahead when the chips were all in.

After the tumult and the shouting had died down, Jones
and Keeler came down to the foyer of the Majestic Hotel,
ready for the taxi that was to take them to Liverpool on the
start of the long journey home. Jack was waiting by the lift to
say farewell. He stepped up to Bobby and held out his hand
and tried to say something, but couldn't. Jones put his arm
around Jack's shoulders and said in a voice that was far from
steady, 'Jack, old man, I'd never have done it without you.
We won it together.' And Jack let go of Jones's hand and sat
right down on the floor of that hotel lobby and began to sob
like a small child.

CHAPTER SEVENTEEN

Mr Jones turns sleuth

In 1948, Tommy Barnes, a fine amateur, played a friendly round with Jones, who was clearly in some discomfort. He mentioned pain in his back and neck. He had some numbness and felt he was losing his strength. As Barnes and the others, Bob Ingram and Henry Lindner, left the eighteenth green, they were thankfully unaware that Jones had played his last round of golf – ever. His problems got worse and an operation on his neck gave little respite. In 1956, with his condition becoming increasingly troublesome, he went to see Dr Houston Merritt at the Columbia-Presbyterian Medical Center in New York, who reached his diagnosis of syringomyelia with a combination of commendable accuracy and profound dismay.

Jones had the misfortune to be stricken with a disease that is best avoided. It consists of an expanding collection of fluid within the spinal cord in the lower part of the neck. The pressure on the nervous tissue of the cord causes relentless and progressive damage affecting the upper and lower limbs.

Muscle wasting, loss of sensation and pain are all substantial problems.

By the late 1950s Jones was struggling to walk despite leg calipers. On his last pilgrimage to St Andrews in 1958 as captain of the American team competing in the Eisenhower Trophy, he moved around the course on a buggy. When receiving the Freedom of St Andrews, he made the few steps to the podium with difficulty, before delivering his moving speech of acceptance. As he left the hall in a buggy, many were unashamedly in tears.

It was in this state of impaired health that he received, in the earlier part of 1958, an enquiry from the secretary of Royal Lytham, Squadron Leader C.W. 'Pincher' Martin. It had been contended by some in Britain that the famous shot he played from sand on the 71st hole of the Open in 1926 had been caught in a photograph (plate 27) but there were doubts about the validity of the claim. A copy of the photograph was sent by Martin to Jones, inviting comment and observation.

There is no preserved copy of the first letter to Jones, but in recent years three subsequent letters of the two-way correspondence have been discovered. They throw fascinating light on the enquiring mind Jones had the good fortune to possess. It can be deduced that the initial letter outlined the belief that the enclosed photograph was indeed of the famous shot and sought Jones's view on the image.

In Jones's reply (figure 2) one can sense how each word has been chosen with care. Given his health, a brief reply indicating that he did not feel it was likely to have been the great shot would have been quite understandable.

Instead he takes on the role of detective, looking at the picture with care and trying to recall the features of a course he had played in competition over 30 years previously and not seen since, apart from a flying visit in the later part of the Second World War. What can be deduced from the position of the ball, the swing and the amount of sand being taken? From what angle was the picture taken? What buildings can be made out? Who else is identifiable?

In his reply, there is insight into the charm and courtesy with which his being was imbued. Referring to the photograph, he starts by saying, 'I wish you would examine it again.' His deprecating reference to 'what you have called "the immortal shot"' is entirely in character. Rather than an abrupt dismissal of the contention, he opens by indicating a willingness to accept it but 'somehow it does not quite ring true to me.'

His first two reasons relate to the technical aspects of the shot and by themselves establish valid and sufficient reasons why this photograph cannot be of the legendary shot, but his third shows a mind full of curiosity. He explores further, indicating that Watrous would have been less visible. It should be borne in mind that at the time of playing the shot, he would have had little or no awareness of where Watrous might have been.

He goes on to suggest that a distant dark building might provide a clue. With magnificent understatement he says, 'my remembrance of the course is naturally not completely fresh.' Since his triumph in the 1926 British Open, his only other visit to St Anne's was in 1944 when, awaiting a flight home, he played several rounds with other US servicemen and with members of the club (an account of this visit is

ROBERT TYRE JONES, JR.
1425 C. & S. BANK BLDG.
ATLANTA, GEORGIA

June 12, 1958

Sqn.-Ldr. C. W. Martin
Royal Lytham & St. Annes Golf Club
St. Annes-on-the-Sea
Lancashire

Dear Sir:

You were very thoughtful indeed to send me
the material relating to the Open Championship and my
Member's Badge, and of course not least, the interesting
photograph.

With respect to the latter, I wish you would
examine it again.

Like you, I should like very much to accept
it as a photograph of what you have called "the immortal
shot", but somehow it does not quite ring true to me.
The reasons are several:

1) My ball was not lying so close to the
bank of the bunker. Had it been, the necessary length
would have been impossible.

2) My ball was lying cleanly, which is quite
obviously not the case in the shot represented by the
photograph.

3) I think you will find if you stand in the
bunker where the marker is now located, Watrous standing
in the fairway would have been at least partially obscured
by mounds.

The dark buildings on the extreme right of
the picture behind the man with his hands in his pockets
looks very much like the corner immediately beyond the
first green. My remembrance of the courss is naturally
not completely fresh, but I am wondering if this shot
could have been played going to the fifth hole.

I am reluctant to trouble you farther, but
have you a small map of the course showing merely the
routing of the holes and the outline of the property?

I shall be watching the tournament with
great interest.

With best wishes to all,

Most sincerely,

Robert T. Jones, Jr.

RTJ:jsm

P.S. - Have you studied the shadow?

Figure 2. Jones's reply of 12 June 1958 to a letter he had received from the
secretary of Royal Lytham and St Anne's.

provided in appendix F). He played so many courses between
1923 and 1958 and his detailed recall of just one, albeit one
that meant so much to him, is remarkable.

His determination to do more than could reasonably
be expected is shown in his next request: 'I am reluctant to
trouble you farther, but have you a small map of the course
showing merely the routing of the holes and the outline of
the property?' Such delightful courtesy was exceptional even
in the period concerned.

It is in his postscript that the most profound insight into the man and his mind is to be seen. In his letter he had already gone further than civility required. One can deduce that the letter was dictated and presented for signature, but meanwhile Jones's eye had perused the photograph once more. He invites the secretary of Royal Lytham to use his own deductive powers and challenges him to do so with the 'P.S. – Have you studied the shadow?'

It can be seen from his reply of the 21 August (figure 3) that the secretary of Royal Lytham rose well to that challenge. Using the shadow as the guide, Pincher Martin reaches his conclusion that the photograph is of Jones playing out of a bunker (now closed) at the former fourteenth hole. His lines of argument are well drawn and, to his mind, resolve the matter fully.

But do they? Watrous is shown as the fellow competitor and Jones did not play with him on previous days. The photograph must therefore have been taken at some point on the final day. From the time sheets it is known that Jones teed off at 9.18am in the morning round and 1.18pm in the afternoon. If the photograph was of the fourteenth hole in the afternoon, the shadow would be to Jones's right-hand side, as the time would by then be after 3pm.

By remarkable good fortune, a different photograph in the 1926 album from the club's archives is of exactly the same shot, taken from a slightly different viewpoint. (plate 28) Watrous and his caddie are not visible but Jones's caddie and the gentleman referred to by Jones as having his hand in his pocket in the first photograph are still seen. There is a pencilled suggestion that this might have been taken on the

21st August, 1958.

R.T. Jones, Jnr.,
1425, C. & S. Bank Buildings,
Atlanta,
Georgia, U.S.A.

Dear Mr. Jones,

Please forgive the long delay in answering your letter of June 12th, but the 'Open' took up so much of my time, and I had a certain amount of investigation to do before I finally decided about the photograph.

However, before starting on the problem of the bunker shot I have a pleasant duty to perform. It is understood that you intend to come over to Britain for the Eisenhower Trophy in October, and I am instructed by the Captain and Council to invite you to pay the Club a visit and if possible dine with them. Many of the Members would like to renew their acquaintanceship with you both from 1926 and the war years, and we can hardly let an opportunity like this slip. May I remind you that we have a Dormy House and can, if necessary, accommodate you overnight.

How very right you were about the shadow. We have successfully proved that the photograph is not that of the famous shot, and further investigation has revealed that it was probably taken in a bunker on the left hand side of the 14th as it was then. The hole faces in exactly the same direction as the 17th, i.e. west, and the back-ground skyline is the same. I had been rather puzzled by the apparent long distance between the bunker and the perimeter of the Course, and had put it down to the effect of a short focus lens in a small camera. However, I stood at the spot yesterday and am now convinced that it was taken at the old 14th. The bunker has now been filled in since the alteration to the Course in 1932 which converted the 14th and 15th into the 15th and made it a par 5.

We do hope that you will be able to visit us once again and see for yourself the alterations which have taken place, but we are still convinced that the Course is still as great as the one you knew and triumphed over.

Yours sincerely,

SECRETARY.

Figure 3. The reply by the secretary, dated 21 August 1958.

fourth hole, but the shadow would not be correct for that hole for either the morning or afternoon round.

The solution that meets Jones's piercing question, 'Have you studied the shadow?' is that the photograph is indeed of Jones playing out of a bunker on the fourteenth and that the shot was played in the morning round. There is no other hole on the course with a similar background of buildings at that time. This deduction is supported by the article in the *Scotsman* of 26 June 1926 which, when describing Jones's back nine in the morning of the final day, states, 'His only slip after that was a bunker at the fourteenth, but he made that good by holing a stiff putt, and so kept the inward column of par figures unbroken.'

Quod erat demonstrandum.

Knowing in hindsight how grim Jones's problems already were in 1958, it is quite revealing to read the understated depictions of his mobility and health. The golf writer Herbert Warren Wind summed Jones up with insight:

> As a young man, he was able to stand up to just about the best that life can offer, which is not easy, and later he stood up with equal grace to just about the worst.

ROBERT TYRE JONES, JR.
1425 C. & S. BANK BLDG.
ATLANTA, GEORGIA

August 27, 1958

Mr. C. W. Martin, Secretary
Royal Lytham & St. Annes Golf Club
St. Annes-on-the-Sea
Lancashire

Dear Mr. Martin:

Thanks very much for your letter of August 21st. I am very glad that you have been able to resolve the question of the photograph.

Your invitation to visit your club is most gracious, and I assure you that I should have great pleasure in accepting, were it likely to be at all possible for me to do so. Unfortunately, my physical mobility is not such that I am able to undertake much moving around. I may even be a little rash in attempting a trip to St. Andrews, but I am very definitely certain that I must limit the excursion to this one purpose. I am therefore planning to fly directly from New York to Prestwick and back, and will be in St. Andrews only for the week including the match.

Please express my gratitude and warm regards to those of your members who were interested in the invitation to me.

Most cordially,

Robert T. Jones, Jr.

RTJ:jsm

Figure 4. Jones's reply of 27 August 1958.

CHAPTER EIGHTEEN

Free, at last!

'Torn to shreds inside, a champion, standing alone on a
mountaintop no one had ever reached before.'

MARK FROST

In 1930, Jones was able, at last, to confront his destiny and, by achieving the apparently unachievable, fulfil it. Each of the four horsemen of the apocalypse was faced down. The British Amateur at St Andrews was an emphatic illustration of Jones's conviction that an outcome could be predetermined. He won the British Open at Hoylake by dogged resolve that overcame the fact that his game was off. At Interlachen, his path to winning the US Open was built on a third round played in a state of serenity. Inevitably, it was at Merion, where he had first made his impact at the age of fourteen in 1916, that he had a surprisingly crisis-free course to winning the US Amateur. It is done.

As Eugene Homans came across the eleventh green at Merion to shake his hand, Jones in victory felt a surge of relief, as years of tension drained from him. Now he could go back to doing what he had yearned to do for more than a decade and play golf for fun. It is clear that championship golf was void of pleasure for Jones. Even his practice rounds were watched by large, smothering galleries. He once said, 'I think I have never felt so lonely as on a golf course in the midst of a championship with thousands of people around, especially when things began to go wrong and the crowds started wandering away.' He liked people, but he preferred them in small doses.

Keeler pointed out that 'Bobby is excessively retiring and even bashful and is embarrassed by strangers staring at him, and acquaintances, or perhaps strangers, coming up and talking with him. He simply dislikes the limelight and is annoyed by it.' A further insight into his nature was given by Ralph McGill who said, 'He is a man who never took himself or his feats seriously enough to stuff his shirt with them. Of them all, his feet are freest of clay, the man himself most devoid of guile, envy, false pride and over-riding ambition.'

Initially championship golf had a buzz but that did not last. Jones pointed out that 'there are two distinct types of golf. Golf – the plain variety – is the most delightful of games, an enjoyable, companionable pastime; tournament golf is thrilling, heartbreaking, terribly hard work – a lot of fun when you are young with nothing on your mind, but fiercely punishing in the end.'

The last time in his life that golf had really been fun was when he was playing in the exhibition matches to help the war effort in the time of the First World War. At one venue he and Perry Adair were each given a bright red Swiss Guard cap and they wore them thereafter. He recalled the time as 'a joy ride for me. I had a world of fun. And when I heard that our combined efforts, mixed foursomes and all, had raised upwards of $150,000 for the Red Cross, I couldn't comprehend it all. It had all been so much fun.'

He sensed that it was when he was aged eighteen, and playing in the 1920 US Amateur at Engineers Club, that the fun evaporated. He noted, 'that was the last of the lighthearted and carefree entertainments golf has served me in what they call the Big Show. After that, the matter became increasingly serious.' By 1923, on his way home from the US Open at Skokie, Keeler asked him what he would do if his game was as poor as O.B.'s. Jones's retort was that he would have a lot more fun out of it. 'And I meant it. This championship quest was getting a bit thick.'

By 1925, he was looking for an equation that would suggest he had met his destiny and could go back to the golf he was missing so much. He confided to Keeler, 'If I could be national champion of the United States six years in succession, either open or amateur, then I'd feel I could hang up the old clubs.' By 1928 he had realised this goal, but the bar had been raised. It was in 1926, when an acute neck pain had interfered with his attempt to win the British Amateur but he had gone on to win the British Open and the US Open, that he had dared to think of winning all four major events – the Opens and Amateurs on both sides of the Atlantic. George Trevor had called this the Impregnable Quadrilateral of golf, while Keeler, borrowing a term from the game of bridge, called it the Grand Slam. Was this the destiny Jones had to meet?

Writing in 1927 and looking back to 1915, he sensed that 'I think I liked competitive golf a good deal better than I do now. All the last year I have been thinking what a wonderful thing it would be to reach the place where I could hang up my clubs and with them the obligations they entail, when used in major competitions.' Anticipating the happy day he mused, 'How will I feel when I read in the papers that the boys are gathering for the national open, or the amateur? It's going to be queer. But there's always one thing to look forward to – the round with Dad and Chick and Brad; the Sunday morning round at old East Lake, with nothing to worry about, when championships are done.'

And now, in 1930, they were done. Privately, he was elated that he could now play golf for fun. Paul Gallico wrote an exquisitely constructed essay in the late 1930s on the impression Jones made on him as a golfer and even more importantly as a man. In repose, Jones was often asked to play with someone he knew only slightly. While others would have coldly spurned such requests, Jones repeatedly made himself available. Gallico recounted how Jones 'would be yanked away from his business to play a round with some impossible and execrable dub who scuffed and sclaffed and shanked and hacked his way around. Patiently Jones would play a round with him, always waiting and hoping for the one good shot that would enable him to bestow the accolade: "Fine shot, partner!" Oh yes, they were always Jones's partner.'

Indeed Gallico, as a young and unknown reporter, was assigned by his paper to play such a round with Jones. Overcome by the occasion, the young man started out playing badly and got steadily worse. He recalled:

I doubt whether I have ever suffered so acutely in all my life. But I learnt something about Jones in that round. Towards the end, having taken nine to get close to the green, I botched my niblick approach, cutting the legs from under the ball instead of hitting it properly, but with astonishing results, because the ball rose into the air, dropped two feet from the pin, and stayed there. Jones sneaked a great sigh of relief and said: 'Fine shot, partner. Well played.'

And then we looked at each other. His face was all properly regulated respect and mingled admiration and serious pleasure at having been permitted to witness such a miraculous demonstration of a difficult game, but there was something funny going on at the corner of his mouth. I guess I must have had a strange expression too, because we suddenly both fell down on the green and howled with laughter, and after that everything was all right.

The response Jones gave to those who wondered how he could tear himself away from the majors was as follows:

What I look forward to now is what I have conceived to be the real way to enjoy golf. To play a lot, never too seriously; to go to all the tournaments in the role of spectator; to play a few rounds in practice with the boys, and then sit back and watch, and perhaps write a bit of stuff if anyone wants to read it; to study the mechanics of the game, to experiment without fear of disturbing

my swing before a championship; to play in charity
matches and minor tournaments if and whenever I like,
but always to leave the big ones to those who are willing
to take the punishment.

Over a dozen years he had taken more punishment than
those who cared about him could bear to watch and they
were relieved when he was able to look around him from
the summit and then step down in contentment. The *New
York Times* eloquently captured the moment, noting, 'With
dignity he quits the memorable scene upon which he nothing
common did or mean.'

What made Gallico rejoice was the aspect that made
Jones different to other sportsmen:

I remember following Jones around many a golf course,
admiring the power of his drives, the startling precision
of his approaches, and the uncanny line and speed of
his putts, and thrilling, likewise, to some of his sub-par
bursts such as five threes in a row at Winged Foot one
year, one of them an eagle on a par-five hole, but I think
I was much more excited at discovering that in Jones I
had at last found a crack performer and a real champion
who had a genuine sense of humor and gift of laughter.

While Jones took his competitive play seriously and played
to win, 'his sense of the ridiculous lay very close to the
surface and I think he saw himself as a slightly comic figure
that did things that amused him vastly. People who are able
successfully to laugh at themselves are able to take a great

amount more of punishment and abuse than the humorless crew. It takes much more to snap the temper of a man who can read something funny into each and every situation.' Gallico's closing line encapsulated his admiration: 'Well, what more can I say for my hero? He was a gentleman and there was laughter in his heart and on his lips, and he loved his friends.'

The moment that defined the legend of Bobby Jones was when, on the links of the Royal Lytham and St Anne's Golf Club, he stood on the penultimate hole and faced his destiny. He plucked his mashie from his bag, quickly took his stance and played a shot of peerless technical excellence, produced under the most intense pressure and exhibiting limitless courage and nerve. What would we give to see his like again?

Bibliography

Blaine, M., *The King of Swings* (Houghton Mifflin, New York 2006)

Cooke, A., *Fun & Games with Alistair Cooke* (Pavilion, London 1994)

Darwin, B., *Golf Between Two Wars* (Chatto & Windus, London 1944)

Darwin, B., *Golfing By-paths* (Country Life, London 1946)

Darwin, B., ed. Peter Ryde, *Mostly Golf – a Bernard Darwin Anthology* (A&C Black, London 1976)

Darwin, B., ed. Robert S. Macdonald, *The Darwin Sketchbook* (Ailsa, Inc. 1991)

Davis, M., *The Greatest of Them All – The Legend of Bobby Jones* (The American Golfer, Inc. 1996)

Eubanks, S., *To Win and Die in Dixie* (Ballantine Books, New York 2010)

Frost, M., *The Grand Slam* (Time Warner, London 2004)

Furber, R., *The Moles 1911–2011: A Byroad in Golfing History* (2011)

Garfield, S., *The Last Journey of William Huskisson* (Faber & Faber, London 2002)

Green, R.G., The Saga of Asgard (Penguin Books, London 1960)

Harrison, G., *Rage of Sand* (Ernest Benn, London 1971)

Jones, R.T. Jnr and Keeler, O.B., *Down the Fairway* (George Allen & Unwin Ltd, London 1927)

Jones, R.T. Jnr, *Golf is My Game* (Chatto & Windus, London 1961)

Jones, R.T. Jnr, *Bobby Jones on Golf* (Cassell & Co., London 1968)

Jones, R.T. Jnr, *Bobby Jones on Golf*. Foreword by Sidney L. Matthew. Introduction by Grantland Rice (Sleeping Bear Press, Chelsea MI 1997. Originally published by One Time Publications 1929)

Keeler, O.B., *The Boys' Life of Bobby Jones Centennial Edition* (Sleeping Bear Press, Chelsea MI 2002 originally published Harper & Brothers 1931)

Keeler, O.B. and Rice, G., *The Bobby Jones Story* (W. Foulsham & Co. Ltd London)

Laney, A., *Following the Leaders* (The Classics of Golf, Ailsa, Inc. 1991)

Leigh, D., *Golf at its Best on the LMS* (1925)

Lewis, C.M., *Bobby Jones and the Quest for the Grand Slam* (Triumph Books, Chicago 2005)

Lewis, C.M., *Considerable Passions – Golf, The Masters and the Legacy of Bobby Jones* (Triumph Books, Chicago 2000)

Matthew, S.L., *Life and Times of Bobby Jones* (Sleeping Bear Press, Chelsea MI 1995)

Miller, R., *Triumphant Journey* (Holt, Rinehart & Winston 1980)

Mortimer, C., and Pignon, F., *The Story of the Open Golf Championship (1860–1950)* (Jarrod, London 1952)

Nickson, E.A., *The Lytham Century and Beyond* (Privately published by the Author 1999)

Prain, E., (ed.), *The Oxford & Cambridge Golfing Society 1898–1948* (Eyre & Spottiswoode, London 1949)

Price, C., (ed.) *The American Golfer* (Random House, New York 1964)

Rapoport, R., *The Immortal Bobby* (John Wiley & Sons, Inc. 2005)

Sarazen, G., *Thirty Years of Championship Golf* (A&C Black, London 1990)

Schupbach, W., *The Paradox of Rembrant's 'Anatomy of Dr. Tulp'* (Wellcome Institute for the History of Medicine 1982)

Steel, D., (ed) *The Golfer's Bedside Book* (B.T. Batsford, London 1971)

Stobbs, J., (compiled by), *At Random Through the Green* (Pelham Books, London 1966)

Van Heel, S.A.C. and others, *Nicolaes Tulp* (Six Art Promotion bv, Amsterdam 1998)

Sources, notes and acknowledgements

Every effort has been made to identify the source of any copyright material, but where items have been obtained from private collections of the club's archives, it has not always been possible to track down the copyright holder, especially where the original source ceased publication long ago. If notified, the publisher will be pleased to acknowledge the use of copyright material in future editions.

All images other than those listed below are from the archives of the Royal Lytham & St Anne's Golf Club or private collections. In the club's archives is an album of photographs, which are reproduced here. It is anticipated that many are being seen for the first time. The photographs are firmly stuck down in the album and it has not been possible to identify by whom they were taken.

The photograph for plate 1 was taken by Aggie McGuiness. The photograph for plate 29 was taken by the author.

The sources of quotations have been indicated in the text where appropriate. Rather than scatter the text with annotations and footnotes, it was resolved to present the story of Jones's victory in the 1926 British Open Championship as a straightforward narrative with a full bibliography of the material from which the story was drawn.

This story is being told in full for the first time, some 86 years after the event, and as a consequence relies heavily on earlier writings. When appropriate some extracts appear as such. The tale of the four rounds is drawn from contemporary newspaper accounts in *The Times*, the *Daily Telegraph*, the *Scotsman*, the *New York Times* and the *Glasgow Herald*.

The Trustees of Royal Lytham & St Anne's Golf Club gave permission to use the photographs and papers in the club's archives. Peter Lewis and Hannah Fleming of the British Golf Museum gave useful and thoughtful advice. Tim Stirk produced the Latin text in chapter 5. Philip Truett made positive observations and helped with details of the Moles Golfing Society. John Lord shared recollections of his uncle who played with Bobby Jones in 1944.

Thanks are due to Henry Lord of Icon Books for taking on the project after its conception and guiding it safely through its pregnancy. Thanks are also due to Robert Sharman of Icon Books for steering the project through the mysteries of the editorial process so that after a far-from-painful labour, there was an exultant birth.

To have a foreword written by Jack Nicklaus is a humbling source of joy and I am most grateful to him and to Scott Tolley, Vice-President of Corporate Communications of the Nicklaus Companies.

Final leader board, 1926 British Open Championship

Mr R.T. Jones, Atlanta (USA)	**72**	**72**	**73**	**74**	**291**
Al Watrous, Grand Rapids (USA)	71	73	69	78	293
Mr G. Von Elm, Rancho (USA)	75	72	76	72	295
Walter Hagen, Pasadena (USA)	68	77	74	76	295
Abe Mitchell, private, St Albans	78	78	72	71	299
Thomas Barber, Cavendish	77	73	78	71	299
Fred Jurado, Lomas (Argentina)	77	76	74	76	301
W. Melhorn, unattached (USA)	70	74	79	80	303
Emmet French, Youngstown (USA)	76	75	74	78	303
H.A. Gaudin, Wanstead	78	78	71	77	304
J.H. Taylor, Mid-Surrey	75	78	71	80	304
T.D. Armour, Congressional (USA)	74	76	75	80	305
R.A. Whitcombe, Came Down	73	82	76	75	306
Tom Williamson, Notts	78	76	76	76	306
Mr W.L. Hartley, Cooden Beach	77	74	79	76	306
H. Walker, Sickleholme	74	77	78	77	306
Fred Robson, Cooden Beach	79	76	77	75	307
Jim Barnes (holder) Rockwood Hall (USA)	77	80	72	78	307
Cyril Walker (USA)	79	71	80	77	307

George Duncan, Wentworth	75	79	80	74	308
Alex Herd, Moor Park	81	76	75	76	308
H.C. Jolly, Foxgrove	79	76	79	75	308
C.A. Whitcombe, Crews Hill	79	78	75	78	310
Joe Kirkwood, Philadelphia (USA)	81	76	78	75	310
and 28 others					

The American entry this year was by some margin the largest of the British Opens played in the 1920s. Of the Americans who qualified for the last day, the last placed was Kirkwood, the trick shot specialist who toured with Hagen playing exhibitions. The only two Americans to miss the halfway cut were the two other amateurs who had played in the Walker Cup, Watts Gunn and Roland McKenzie.

The course at St Anne's then and now

For those familiar with the course of today over which the British Open and other events are played, it may be of interest to compare the course played by Jones and the others in 1926 with the modern layout. Harry Colt had made substantial changes over a number of years between 1919 and 1925. The major changes compared with today are of distance but there are significant differences at nine holes – the current first, fourth, seventh, eleventh, twelfth, thirteenth, fourteenth, fifteenth and eighteenth.

The club is fortunate in having a detailed survey from 1934, which establishes the course then in play, and the changes between 1926 and 1934 are well documented.

In 1926 the tee for the **first hole** was near the corner of the current practice putting green nearest to the front door of the Dormy House and the green was practically encircled by a necklace of bunkers. The yardage was 223 yards. At that time, players were using hickory-shafted clubs. It is quite startling to learn that they were taking irons from the tee.

Apart from changes in yardage, the **second and third holes** were much as they are today with a somewhat different pattern of bunkering. Anticipating the 1926 Open, Darwin commented how the second and third had until then been 'quite pleasant and required reasonable accuracy, but yet they were comparatively anaemic. They are full-blooded holes today, for there is a terrifying carry from the second tee, and the third green has been carried on into some admirable hilly country.' The new third green was some seventy yards beyond the earlier one. Played from the same tee as today, the **fourth hole**, which now measures 393 yards, was in 1926 only 343 yards and played in a dead straight line. From the configuration of the ground there is an impression that the old green was off the right of the current fairway, nearly level with the front of the fifth tee.

The **fifth hole** was as it is today. Looking forward to the 1926 Open, Darwin recalled that 'the fifth I remember as a rather mild, easy short hole in a dell. It is anything but mild now, for the flag is perched on a narrow, guarded and defiant plateau, waiting to be won.' The yardage of the **sixth hole** was 431 yards and the green considerably smaller than the present one. Facing the drive at the **seventh hole** were four bunkers running across the ridge some 120 yards off the tee and a line of bunkers then ran up either side of the fairway. Overall, some 26 bunkers sought to catch the errant drive. The green was of a punchbowl design some fifty yards short of and to the right of the current green, which was only created as recently as 2009. The **eighth hole and ninth hole** are unchanged. The ninth baffled Jones on each of his four rounds and on three occasions he dropped a stroke there.

The green at the **tenth hole** was in the vicinity of the tee for the eleventh hole that is some forty yards to the south of the tenth green, so the pitch was played over the corner of the hill now on the left edge of the tenth fairway. The tee for the **eleventh hole** was on the other side of the public pathway behind the current tenth green. From there the hole ran for 601 yards in a dead straight line to a green in the vicinity of the current twelfth green. Playing into the prevailing wind, this was apparently a dreary hole with no redeeming virtues.

The **twelfth hole** was a straight hole of 291 yards played from the current ladies' tee for today's thirteenth hole to the present thirteenth green. The **thirteenth hole** was the fourteenth hole of today, though there were no houses of any kind on the inland aspect of the course. The **fourteenth hole** ran from the current fifteenth tee to a green that can still be made out just after the substantial hollow some 320 yards out. This hollow was formerly the punchbowl to that green on the course laid out by George Lowe in 1896. The length of the hole in 1926 was 343 yards.

The **fifteenth hole** was played from a tee in the area that now has the fifth tee on the neighbouring 'short course' to the current fifteenth green. It was a short hole with a yardage of 184 yards. The **sixteenth hole** was much as it is today. Reference has been made in the body of the book to the discovery of the unusual way in which the course was prepared. Huge areas had the turf and grass ripped away leaving vast expanses of sandy wastes. It was in one of these areas that Jones drove his ball at the **seventeenth hole** in his last round, from where he played his unforgettable shot that won the championship. Since 1926 the exposed sandy areas have once again grassed over and the bunkering pattern has evolved over time. The **eighteenth hole** is now 413 yards but then was only 349 yards and while the first line of diagonal bunkers Colt introduced existed then, the second line on the left part of the fairway some way further on did not. There was a bunker behind the back of the green that was introduced to replace a flowerbed that had previously been there. This was the bunker Hagen found when playing his last hole.

Summing up the links, Darwin said, 'I think that St. Anne's is essentially a course for the big battalions, and that one of them will win. On the course everything has been tightened up. St. Anne's is a fine, long, difficult course, and the man is not born who can play four rounds of it without getting into bunkers.'

In 1926 the holes still bore names, though these have since faded from use. The yardage from that time can be compared with that of today:

	1926	Today
1. The Pond	223	206
2. The Cabin	423	481
3. The Railway	452	477
4. The Clubhouse	343	391
5. The Clifton	190	218
6. The Trap	431	494
7. The Long Out	543	589
8. The Path	387	417
9. The Monkey	161	164
Front nine	3,153	3,437
10. Tribulation	301	385
11. Long In	601	601
12. Plantation	313	196
13. Boundary	447	357
14. Mugliston	352	443
15. Westward Ho!	184	464
16. Gap	347	358
17. Ridge End	411	467
18. Home	349	410
Back nine	3,305	3,681
Total	**6,458**	**7,118**

Appendix C

Bobby Jones and the Claret Jug puzzle

Before addressing the Claret Jug Puzzle, the appropriate name for the course and the mystery of the apostrophe warrant consideration.

From its earliest days, the course over which the 1926 Open was contested was referred to as 'St. Anne's' by writers such as Darwin and Hutchinson. Jones himself consistently wrote about 'St. Anne's'. Since the Second World War the tendency has been to refer instead to 'Royal Lytham' or just 'Lytham' and nowadays the only time the blessed Saint Anne is mentioned is when the full current title of Royal Lytham and St Annes is used, lamentably without an apostrophe.

To apostrophise or not to apostrophise? That is the question. Neither Darwin nor Jones was in any doubt: the apostrophe had to be there. The town was named after the Parish Church of St Anne and indeed the church carrying her name existed before the town was created in the years after 1874 following the formation of the land holding company.

There was the apostrophe in the name of the company, the St Anne's-on-the-Sea Land Holding Company, and in the name of the town, St Anne's-on-the-Sea. In Gabriel Harrison's book *Rage of Sand*, the definitive account of the creation of the town, St Anne's-on-the-Sea carries her apostrophe with pride throughout.

On 27 February 1886 the Lytham and St Anne's Golf Club was formed and the apostrophe persists through the early years, so it would appear that the answer is clear. The apostrophe should be there. The waters get muddied in 1926 when the club received the following letter:

Home Office
Whitehall

B25,012
15th May 1926

I am directed by the Secretary of State to inform you that he has laid before the King your application of 11th instant on behalf of the Council of the Lytham and St. Annes Golf Club for permission to use the prefix "Royal" in the name of the Club and that His Majesty has been graciously pleased to Command that the Club shall henceforth be known as the "Royal Lytham and St. Annes Golf Club".

I am,
Sir,
Your obedient servant

W.G. Allen

The Secretary
Lytham and St. Annes Golf Club
St. Annes-on-the-Sea.

Three matters of interest are generated by this letter. The first is that the permission to include the word Royal was only granted a little over a month before the Open was to be played. The second is the use of the word 'and' rather than '&' in the Command of the King as to how the club was henceforth to be known, which therefore applies to the present time. The third is the lamentable absence of the apostrophe. So should the apostrophe be used now or not? Should the answer reflect the usage of the time when the club was founded, current usage or the enduring Command of the Monarch?

In 1960 Jones wrote to the captain of the day, Leighton Treasure, thanking him for 'your gracious letter and one of your club ties.' In his concluding paragraph he says, 'You may be sure I often think of St. Annes – not only of the championship there, but also of the great pleasure I had in visiting there on my way back from France during the war. I have been delighted to follow the continuing contributions of the club to the game of golf.' Not an apostrophe in sight. By that stage of his illness, his letters were typed by his trusty secretary Jean Marshall and perhaps it can be surmised that her diligence about apostrophes was less than that of Jones himself.

ROBERT TYRE JONES, JR.
FOURTH FLOOR HAAS-HOWELL BUILDING
ATLANTA 3, GEORGIA

September 14, 1960

F. Leighton Treasure, Esq.
Royal Lytham & St. Annes Golf Club
St. Annes-on-the-Sea
Lancashire, England

Dear Mr. Treasure:

Alex Barker favored me with a most delightful
visit the other day and brought with him your
gracious letter and one of your club ties. I want
you to know that I am most grateful for your thought.

Your news of the placque and the competition
for my iron gave me much pleasure. I am so happy
that the club has put this old implement to such use.
I am afraid that it has thus acquired a dignity far
beyond its worth.

You may be sure that I often think of St. Annes –
not only of the championship there, but also of the
great pleasure I had in visiting there on my way back
from France during the war. I have been delighted to
follow the continuing contributions of the club to the
game of golf.

With all good wishes and many thanks,

Most sincerely,

Robert T. Jones, Jr.

RTJ:jsm

cc: Mr. Alex Barker

Figure 5. The letter from Jones to the club, dated 14 September 1960.

The second question to be addressed was whether or not the location of Jones's first British Open victory was adorned in the engraving on the Claret Jug with an apostrophe. Those who favour the presence of the apostrophe will be saddened to learn that on the original Claret Jug the location is given as St. Annes, again with not an apostrophe in sight.

The Claret Jug puzzle

The full line for that year reads: 'Mr. R.T. Jones Jr, Atlanta, USA 1926 at St. Annes 291 strokes' and in smaller italic print below is added an extra line '*(Amateur)*'.

Jones was the third and last amateur to win the British Open and as the word 'amateur' appeared in brackets after the names of the other two, John Ball and Harold Hilton, it is entirely consistent that it should appear after the name of Jones. It is a happy coincidence that all three amateurs who won the British Open were members of Royal Lytham & St Anne's. Hilton was a subscribing member and he and Ball played for the club on many occasions against opposition such as the Oxford & Cambridge Golfing Society and Seaton Carew. Ball played there for many years and with Hilton plundered many of the gold medals and silver iron competitions. Ball was an Honorary Member of the club, as was Bobby Jones.

But why the mention of Atlanta? Although the country of origin is no longer engraved, it was in the years concerned and the element USA is understandable. What is less easily explained is the presence of the word Atlanta. American winners in the years before and immediately after 1926 are simply engraved as 'J.M. Barnes, USA' or 'Walter Hagen, USA' but in each of the three years when Jones won, Atlanta is mentioned.

The considered conclusion of Hannah Fleming of the British Golf Museum at St Andrews is that 'This stylistic decision may have been made by the engraver himself or perhaps the committee decided that it would be more accurate.'

Matters being decided on the whim of the engraver may also explain the engravings relating to subsequent winners here. In 1952 the location has changed from 'St. Annes' to 'Royal Lytham and St. Annes' and remained so for subsequent Opens up to and including 1974, sometimes appearing as 'Royal Lytham & St. Annes' but never with an apostrophe. At times the engraver has struggled and on one occasion found himself spilling over onto a second line. Overall this was manageable unless the winner had a long name.

In 1979 the winner was Severiano Ballesteros! Perhaps without asking anyone, the engraver that year reverted to St. Annes, and it has been St. Annes in all Opens since then. Infuriatingly without an apostrophe.

Appendix D

Tommy Armour on Jones

In 1935 Tommy Armour, one of the leading professional golfers of the late 1920s and early 1930s, wrote a series of 'Penshots' about golfers he knew for *The American Golfer* magazine. No. 6 was about Bobby Jones and revealed the admiration the Scot had for the young Georgian. The two men would often play together in the winters of 1925/26 and 1926/27. Their matches were fiercely competitive and played a significant role in sharpening up Jones's game.

Armour's account of these matches is revealing:

> Bob and I used to play a lot of golf together. Our friendly matches almost invariably were generous, pleasant little affairs. Yes, just like the Dempsey–Firpo fight. By the fourth hole we were not talking to each other. We played to the finish in silence as heavy as that of the half-a-minute-before-the-zero-hour. But when the game was ended and we were in the locker room engaged in that happy rite having to do with the disposal of the

mellow Georgia corn unlaxer, hostilities were forgotten in the most delightful moments I've ever spent in golf clubhouses.

He was impressed with the concentration Jones brought to those conflicts and he wrote:

> I started those games that ended in silence by ribbing Bob about his golf and chattering to see for myself if anything ever could puncture the battleplate of Bob's concentration. I don't think there is. When we played together and Bob was intent on turning in the sort of performance one expects as the divine right of the King, Jones knew no diverting thought had a place. That's why, I'm confident, he wouldn't talk to me after a few holes and give me openings to disturb him.

Whatever Armour thought of Jones as a golfer, he thought more of him as a man, starting his article by stating, 'Southern gentleman, new style, is Bob Jones. In this scheme of things entire, Bob, beyond doubt, is even greater as exhibit A of the high type of young Southern gentleman than he is great as a golfer.' In contrast to the total concentration Jones showed in matches that mattered, Armour admired the way Jones accompanied ordinary mortals around a course, noting that 'Bob will play with fellows who have 15 handicaps by the grace of charity and five superbly lucky games, and keep a cheery, relaxing chat with them all the way around the course.'

The article also revealed the consideration and kindness Jones showed to others. Armour wrote:

One of the finest things about Bob's concentration is the manner in which it works in with his graciousness. I remember an instance of this at the Rolyat Hotel at Pasadena, Florida, during the boom days. Bob was there playing an exhibition with Hagen. Hagen gave Bob a robust beating – a trimming so strong that it, to me, was evidence enough that Bob was thinking more of his real estate interests than of his golf at the time. During an evening down there at least seven people who were strangers to Bob came in and sat around the throne room. Jones was introduced to them once and when other visitors came in Bob, in doing the honours, introduced the newcomers to each of the strangers by name. That always has impressed me because I am like most men in finding it difficult to remember one name, and then only after it has been repeated several times.

Armour also gave an insight into a foible of Jones that has since been forgotten. He revealed that 'A quiet laugh that Jones has always given me is the depth of superstition about his golf apparel. When he started a championship playing well, he'd wear the same shirt, sweater, knickers, shoes and stockings until the championship was completed. I'd like to have the old clothes he wore in 1930. Maybe it was a breeze from the follow-through of those knickers that skipped one of his topped shots across the ninth at Interlachen during the National Open a few years back. Chances are, though, that Bob's luck then and at other times was on the same order as to the Civil War general who said the Lord is on the side that has the most guns.'

Armour summed up his friend thus:

By this time you'll have the hunch that I rate Bob Jones
as the top of fine young men. I do; but that's only half
of the story. Of all the fellows who have ever played
golf, Jones is the most ruthless, ravenous destroyer. In
competition out on Allah's beautiful green footstool,
beneath Allah's bright sky, Jones strained the quality of
mercy so fine there wasn't enough mercy left to be seen
by a microscope that could make an atom loom up like
Gibraltar. The reason is plain and nothing against Jones.
He concentrated on playing the game. The game is for
someone to win and someone to lose – no scoreless ties
about it, in the Jones plan. Jones went after them all
with the idea of winning by 10 and 8, or by 40 strokes.

He concluded, 'Thinking back on how good he was when
he was concentrating on competition, I am puzzled that
he didn't beat the opposition by those margins. The only
answer I have is that his good manners must have softened
his concentration.'

Whatever impact this article might have made in 1935,
it does not appear to have attracted any attention since.
For someone who liked Jones to describe him as 'the most
ruthless, ravenous destroyer' gives a piercing insight into
the competiveness and concentration Jones brought into
an encounter.

The Berrie portrait

Jones made his last trip to play competitive golf in Britain in 1930, winning the British Amateur at St Andrews and the British Open at Hoylake on his way to the 'Impregnable Quadrilateral' or Grand Slam. Agreed On the Wirral, the qualifying round was played at nearby Wallasey. To mark his visit there, an ex-captain of Wallasey, Mr E.B. Royden, commissioned the Liverpool artist and Wallasey member, J.A.A. Berrie to produce a painting of Jones. This was the first time Jones had sat for a portrait in Britain and Royden presented it to Wallasey as a reminder of Jones's visit. Jones was very taken with the painting and commissioned Berrie to paint one for his own home. He also signed the one that still hangs in the Wallasey clubhouse.

Berrie was at that time the area's leading portrait and landscape painter. As a student he had learnt his craft under the tutelage of Marmaduke Flower, Marcel Beranneau and Senor Casteluchio. He was elected to RCA in 1923 and became an FRSA in 1950. In later life his subjects included

King George V, Queen Mary, King Edward VIII, George VI, Elizabeth II, Winston Churchill and Admiral Earl Mountbatten of Burma. Today, the interior of the Artists' Club in Eberle Street, Liverpool affords evidence that he was much in demand locally. He spent his later years in Nairobi and in the Killarney area of Johannesburg. The portrait Royden commissioned showed Jones from the waist up, wearing a V-neck pullover. After the sitting was finished, Jones removed the blue sweater he was wearing and gave it to a Wallasey member, who then put it on to sit for Berrie in order that the painting from the neck down could be completed. Before leaving the studio, Jones signed and dated the lower right-hand corner of the canvas.

John R. Dixon was captain of Royal Lytham & St Anne's in 1926 but illness prevented him from attending the presentation and giving the Claret Jug to Jones. After 1930, Dixon commissioned Berrie to produce another portrait of Jones and presented it to his own club, where it is on display in the Club Room. Reproduced in the plate section (plate 1), it shows Jones nearly full length, with his driver 'Jeannie Deans' in the crook of his left arm. When Clifford Roberts of the Masters first saw this painting, he commented that it captured the essence of Jones better than any other portrait he had ever seen.

In 1953, Jones wrote to Royden, by then Sir Ernest B. Royden, Baronet, recalling the sitting, during which 'Mr. Berrie kept me occupied for not more than thirty minutes and during that time pleasantly refreshed with a whiskey and soda. As an object lesson in painless portraiture, this was the best I have ever seen.' He pointed out that 'as a matter of

ROBERT T. JONES, JR.
1425 C. & S. Bank Building
ATLANTA, GEORGIA

March 17, 1953

Sir Ernest B. Royden, Bt.,
Hill Bark, Frankby,
West Kirby, England.

My dear Sir Ernest,

        I remember the portrait done of me by Mr. John A. A. Berrie. As a matter of fact, of a number of portraits done of me, I have always liked his best, although of course I would swap none of them for the one the President has recently finished.

        Unfortunately I have not been back to Hoylake nor Wallasey since 1930, but I have seen one of Mr. Berrie's portraits of me in the Lytham-Saint Anne's Club, and also have a copy of the Wallasey portrait in my home, where it always attracts attention and admiration.

        Again on the issue of "The Times" which you so graciously mention, Mr. Berrie kept me occupied for not more than thirty minutes and during that time pleasantly refreshed with a whiskey and soda. As an object lesson in painless portraiture, this was the best I have ever seen.

        It was good to hear from you and if you see or communicate with Mr. Berrie, I wish you would give him my warm regards.

        Most sincerely,

        Robert T. Jones, Jr.

P. S. - I forgot to tell you that the portrait done by the President was based upon a golfing photograph taken of me about 1930, but the President has never seen Mr. Berrie's portrait.

Figure 6. Jones's letter of 17 March 1953 (his birthday) to Sir Ernest Royden about the Berrie portrait.

fact, of a number of portraits done of me, I have always liked his best.' Although he had a copy of the Wallasey portrait in his home, his departure after the Open at Hoylake meant he never saw the original completed, though as he mentions in his letter (figure 6) 'I have seen one of Mr. Berrie's portraits in the Lytham-Saint Anne's Club.'

Just one more time – Jones visits St Anne's in 1944

It was entirely fitting that the last round of golf Jones ever played in the British Isles should be at St Anne's.

There was no need for Jones to volunteer for active service when, in the aftermath of Pearl Harbor, America entered the Second World War. He had held an Army reserve commission since 1931 and following the debacle of Pearl Harbor he asked his reserve unit commander about possible service. Bearing in mind his age, his having a wife and family and his previous vein surgery, he was encouraged to stay at home and use his celebrity status to raise money for the war effort.

To Jones this seemed unreasonable. It was, after all, just what he had done in his teens when he was too young to enlist. There is a perception that he subsequently felt uncomfortable that while he was enjoying playing golf exhibitions with Perry Adair, those just a few years older were putting their lives at risk for their country.

Accordingly he was commissioned a Captain in the US Army in June 1942. The threat of a German air strike on the eastern seaboard was real and, following the humiliation of Pearl Harbor, Jones and others took their work organising an air defence seriously. By 1943 that threat had faded and Jones was transferred to the 84th Fighter Wing of the Ninth Tactical Command, receiving training *inter alia* as a prisoner-of-war interrogator. In England he played his part as an intelligence officer in the preparation of the Normandy invasion. His unit's task was to devise plans to bomb bridges over the river Seine.

With his unit, he landed in Normandy the day after the main invasion and found himself in a foxhole for some hours under sporadic German artillery fire. During that experience, he may have wished that he had followed his unit commander's recommendation! He remained with his unit in France for some months, addressing legal matters in Paris and being promoted first to Major and then to Lieutenant-Colonel. He then received word that his father was ill. He requested permission to return home and was flown home via BAD2, the American airbase in Warton, Lancashire.

Having the best part of a week to wait there for his flight out, he answered the siren call of the links at St Anne's, less than five miles away. One evening he and the club's professional Tom Fernie played with other US servicemen by playing three holes with one pair then dropping back to play another three holes with the pair behind.

On another day he played a match in aid of the Red Cross against J.C. Bradbury. The stake being played for was £1 and on losing, Jones not only handed over the £1 note but also signed it with an indication of the occasion. Not surprisingly it became a treasured possession in the Bradbury household, framed and displayed on the mantlepiece. To play, Jones borrowed the clubs of another club member, Donald Beaver, who was away on active service.

Current member John Lord recalls his aunt's response to the advice of an American serviceman, Tom Madden, to her in 1944, when she failed to get out of a bunker on the eighteenth. He said, 'Keep your head down' and she feistily responded, 'Mind your own damned business.' From that unpromising start romance bloomed and she later married him. One evening he was accosted by the St Anne's professional, Tom Fernie, who said, 'A fellow countryman of yours is looking for a game and you might like to play with him. His name is Bobby Jones.' Madden did indeed play with Jones the following afternoon, describing it as a delightful experience, and caddied for Jones the next day when he played in an exhibition. Plate 30 shows Jones in uniform standing before the Berrie portrait.

Index

Interlachen Country Club 73
Inwood Golf Club 54
Isherwood, A. J. 133

Jamieson, Andrew 63, 82–6, 137–8, 210
Jeannie Deans (driver) 107
Johnston, Harrison R. 63
Johnston, Jimmy 74
Jones, Clara (Bobby's mother) 6, 71, 74
Jones, Robert Permedus (Bobby's father) 4, 5–7
Jones, Robert Tyre (Bobby)
  birth 6
  early life 3–12
Jones, Robert Tyre (Bobby's grandfather) 4–5
Jones, Rowland 108
Jones, William Bailey (Bobby's brother) 6
Jurado, Jose 120, 125, 126

Kant, Immanuel 14
Keeler, Oscar Bane 'Pop' 11–12, 15, 27–8, 35–6, 41, 47, 49, 60–61, 68–9, 71, 72–3, 82, 83, 85, 106–7, 115–16, 134, 175, 178–9, 192, 198, 208, 209–10, 211–12, 224, 225
Keffer, Karl 142
Kerrigan, Tommy 36
Kirby 159
Kirkwood, Joe 102, 172

Ladies Amateur Championship 97
Ladies Golf Union (LGU) 95
Ladies' Course 122
Laney, Al 49–50, 186, 190–92, 202–4
law school 9
Layton 80–81
lean years 41–3

Leigh, Dell 99
Lindner, Henry 213
Lockhart, Gordon 2
long driving championship (1926) 122–7
Long Island 20, 49, 140–41
Low, John 98
Lowe, George 95, 97
Lytham 91–2
Lytham & St Anne's Golf Club 92–103, 117–19, 120–21
  see also British Open, 1926 (St Anne's)

Macbeth, Norman 98
Macfarlane, Charles 109–10, 209–10
Mackenzie, Roland 78, 81, 120, 126
Maiden, Stewart 'Kiltie' 7
Majestic Hotel 174–5, 212
Manford, G. C. 30
Martin, Sqn Ldr C. W. 'Pincher' 214, 216–21
Matthew, Sidney L. 47–8
McGill, Ralph 224
McIntire, Jack 211–12
McLeod, Fred 21, 139–40, 152, 166–7, 168, 172, 176
megaphone incident, US Amateur (1919) 59
Melhorn, Wild Bill 89, 138–9, 154–5, 164–5, 168, 172, 176
Meredith, Owen, Earl of Lytton 15
Merion Golf Club 17–18, 47, 62, 64, 73–4, 134, 223
middle name (Tyre) 4
Miller, T. H. 95
Milwaukee Sentinel 81
miners' strike, Britain 1926 78–9
Minikhada Club 63
Mitchell, Abe 88–90, 102–3, 121, 156, 167, 170, 176